In Your Face

In Your Face
Duchenne Muscular Dystrophy

...All Pain...All GLORY!

Alaskan Mom's Journey With Son's Deadly Disease

By Misty VanderWeele

ISBN 978-0-615-35758-4

Edited by: Mindy Cameron

Cover Design by: KillerCovers

Cover Photography by Jay Johnson of Healing Life Touch Photography

For my favorite son, Luke

"Believe that there's light at the end
of the tunnel.
Believe that you may be that light for
someone else" ~KOBI YAMADA

Contents

FOREWORD

"In Your Face" is a true life journey of tremendous love, hope, continuous heart break, silent pain and the cherished mystery of life. A candid story that is both the worst and the best thing that has ever happened to me. A story of transformation that started when my son Luke was only four years old.

On a sunny Alaskan July day, life as I knew it changed in 9 words. Words that no parent should ever have to hear. Words I'll never forget: "I am sorry, your son has Duchenne Muscular Dystrophy." The pain was deafening in my ears, my entire world was spinning. My mind was screaming NO! Not my little boy! In an instant I went from dreams of sports, bicycles, outdoor hunting and fishing, snowmobiling and most of the outdoor Alaskan lifestyle, to living in the face of the possibility of my son's early death.

If you have ever watched the Jerry Lewis MDA Labor Day Telethon, you have heard of Duchenne Muscular Dystrophy or (DMD). DMD or just Duchenne as I like to call it, is the most common life threatening form Muscular Dystrophy (MD) and is often confused with MS. Duchenne is considered a genetic muscle wasting disorder. Typically Duchenne boys are diagnosed before age 5. They noticeably fatigue easily and find it challenging keeping up with others their age as their muscles swell and joints become restricted. The simplest of tasks like holding a pencil or rolling over in bed become difficult and eventually impossible. Most Duchenne boys need a wheelchair between ages of 10-12. As they get older and Duchenne progresses the heart and breathing muscles become compromised and begin to fail. Sadly most boys with Duchenne have not survived their teens. Duchenne affects about 1 in 3500 boys, nearly 20,000 born each year around the world.

Duchenne is caused by a gene mutation on the X chromosome and that is why the disease almost exclusively affects males. Females have two X chromosomes and so if the Duchenne causing mutation occurs in one, the other compensates for the fault. Women carry the defective gene but almost never manifest the symptoms to a deadly degree. Carriers have a 50 percent chance of passing along the defective gene to their male offspring and since males don't have another X chromosome to compensate for the fault, they develop the disease. The daughters of carrier women have a 25 percent chance of being carriers themselves.

Those with Duchenne appear normal at birth but are usually rendered to a wheelchair by their early teens as the disease progresses. At the time of Luke's diagnosis over 14 years ago before the internet, I was told that Duchenne boys usually pass away during their teen years. The last few years, however, that outlook has changed somewhat as many Duchenne boys are living several years longer, some even into their early 30s.

My son Luke is now 18 and is considered to be in the last phase of the disease because he is in a wheelchair full time and requires respiratory and cardiac therapy.

I have gone from "Why God why?" to "Thank you Luke for honoring me in choosing me as your mother." I believe that each and every one of us choose our parents before being born here on this planet. It is the only explanation that makes sense to me, because in my book no loving God would make or cause this sort of pain in anyone's life especially that of a little child.

The one thing that stands fast is that although Luke hasn't been cured, he has lived longer than "they" told me he would. There have been times that I thought I would die from the pain of it all and times of complete and utter bliss. The many angels who have crossed our path in the form of teachers, journalists, doctors, nurses, therapists, family, friends, care providers and complete strangers I wouldn't have known otherwise. Life is such a mystery and I don't want to miss any of it!

I am writing In Your Face during Luke's senior year in high school as a gift to him for graduation. I think completing 12 years of education is an accomplishment for any 18-year-old, but especially for a Duchenne boy who has triumphed in the face of death. I am writing it as a way to preserve the essence of our sacred journey of unknown length together. To have something tangible that will go on and help others long after his passage to heaven. With that being said, now I know why parents write memoirs after their children pass. I had no idea about the amount of energy writing would take and the emotion I would expend while still living every day and providing Luke care and sound advice so that he is able to go on and advocate for himself and deal with his medical condition.

When I sat down to write this book, I realized that I remembered the past in sort of a dream-like consciousness. I don't know if we all remember our pasts like this or whether my memory is trying to help me distance myself from the horror of watching my boy's body being ravaged by Duchenne. I thought long and hard about how I was going to be able to tell my story in an uplifting positive way without being consumed by the pain as I relived the good, the bad and the ugly imprint Duchenne has tried to force upon me. I especially want to make sure I convey how I have had to change my internal belief system and the way I perceived everything about who I am and about life in general to not only survive, but thrive. My entire mission is to weave what is a very sad human circumstance into threads of hope to inspire a

Duchenne Movement. People not knowing that 20,000 boys a year are being diagnosed with Duchenne who some have considered a death sentence, is not acceptable!

Since memory comes back to us in flashes of conversations, tidbits of recollection and the emotional impact that past events have upon us, instead of one continuous thread, I started each Chapter with a titled introduction then titled memory segments that follow Luke's progression of Duchenne. Eventually ending with an entire chapter dedicated to anyone who is touched by Duchenne wanting to join the Duchenne Movement or at least wear the t-shirt. You can find out more about me and pick up a free guide for "THRIVING" In The Face of Duchenne at http://MistyVanderweele.com.

Some of the names have been changed as some of the issues and challenges often involved a group of individuals and not always in the most positive of ways. I am extremely happy that I was able to use a lot of real names, as many of the people in this story have been very supportive. Many heartfelt tears have been shed during the creation of this book and I wouldn't change that for the world. After all life is meant to be felt and *lived!*

From the beginning I, like every other mother out there, didn't want to miss one smile, one tear, one struggle, or one triumph of my child's life. What other choice does a mother have when the reality of her child's probable death is so IN YOUR FACE?

Preface by Debra Miller

T he very first book of the Bible depicts a story about Abraham's nephew, Lot, who was kidnapped by the enemy. When Abram (Abraham) heard that his nephew had been taken captive, he called out his army of trained men and went in pursuit. During the night Abram attacked the enemy. He recovered all the goods and brought back his nephew, Lot and ALL his possessions. (Genesis chapter 14:14-14:16) "In Your Face" is a story about a remarkable young man, Luke, the love of his mother and the call to action that is the result of her love and her faith. It's a safe assumption that Abraham was in constant prayer with God, but he didn't stop there. He also took action and stepped out in faith to save his nephew. Misty VanderWeele is building a different kind of "army," an army of parents, patients and advocates that aren't content to let others decide the future for those they love, that are afflicted with Duchenne muscular dystrophy.

The small town in Alaska where Luke and Misty live is about as isolated as you can get from the hubs of science and support groups. Perhaps Misty's self reliance is enhanced by this distance since she had to find her own way in dealing with Duchenne.

Whatever the cause, Misty sets an example for all families that have had their dreams for their child's future shattered. She did not shelter her son from living a full life, in fact, Luke has had the benefit of the great outdoors and is getting ready for college next year.

None of us really know what we are capable of until the need arises. If we get lulled into thinking that the "experts" will take care of our children then we are short changing our children and ourselves by not experiencing the deep satisfaction that comes with knowing you are working toward the solution. Those who have taken action, whether it be local fund raising or advocacy, have started a chain reaction of events and contacts that will move us much closer to a cure for Duchenne.

When our son was diagnosed with Duchenne seven years ago, we knew that this disease was much bigger than we were and that our son was truly in God's hands. We noticed a tendency among some other DMD parents we met to put their faith in people they believed had the answers, whether it be organizations, science or medicine. But as Abraham showed, God gives us opportunities to act and help others.

"In Your Face" is a perfect title for this book. Misty has taken the gloves off and has posed a challenge to everyone to be part of the cure for Duchenne. She is a perfect example of a mom who has recognized the power of the individual and she offers solutions and encouragement to families everywhere. Very few people ever hear the word Duchenne until someone close to them is diagnosed. Until the public knows about this disease, it will remain underfunded for research and care. Misty knows this and is stepping outside the box to get the word out about Duchenne.

We don't know what the future holds for our boys that have Duchenne, but we do know that everyone affected with this disease has a responsibility to contribute what they can to change the outcome. Everyone has something to add. Misty didn't train to be an author but when she saw the need she rose to the occasion.

Misty and Luke's journey is an extraordinary story of love, determination and bravery. If Misty had analyzed her experience and skill set to determine if, or what she should do to help boys with Duchenne, it's very possible she'd still be pondering that list. She realized that there just wasn't enough time to do that, and she took the first step. When you read this book, I hope you will be as inspired as I am by Misty's determination.

To Misty with gratitude from another parent of a boy with Duchenne,

Debra Miller
President and Founder
CureDuchenne

Acknowledgments

First thank you to Luke Delia for being my son. You are my light at the end of the tunnel. Thank you Jenna VanderWeele for being the best daughter a mother could ask for. Remember your love and sensitivity is *your* gift. Thank you to my husband Glen VanderWeele, you make my life sing, I swell with love and awe witnessing your love for my son. Thank you to Patrick Delia for standing by your son's side when many dad's don't, also thank you for your often times stubborn, quiet, unbending streak which has pushed me to the max to be a better me and the mother I am today. Thank you to my little sister Autumn Tweedy. My life is sweeter when you're in it. Know that your love and encouragement in writing this book has helped to keep me going. Thank you to my little brother Boone Tanner. I had no idea I was your hero until you told me. Not sure when that happened, but I'll take it. Thank you to my mother Raylene Getts, I honor you for our sacred mother-daughter path we are taking together, it is no accident that you are my mom. Thank you to my "daddy Mike" for being my childhood fantasy, my night in shinning armor, the feather story and not climbing on that whale. Thank you to my step dad Doug Tanner, you are the dad that showed up, giving me just what I needed to survive and thrive. Thank you Mary Krall my grandmother for showing me that living in dysfunction is a choice you don't have to live, our memories together permeate my daily life. Thank you to my wonderful mother-in-law Suus VanderWeele, your shoulder has been a huge blessing, your guidance is treasured beyond measure. Thank you and Namesta to Raymond a Patricia Veenkant for showing me possibilities, your belief in me and the mystery of life is one of the greatest gifts I have ever received. To my dearest friend Kelly Caraway and her wonderful husband Tim, thank you for the unconditional, genuine love, friendship and honesty you give me and my family. Also Kelly thank you for being my sounding board more times than I can remember. Thank you to all of you who gave me permission to use your real names. You are the reason that this story can be told, the wind beneath my wings to carry on. Thank you to everyone who has ever worked with Luke or been on his support team from pre-school, high school and onward. Thank you to all of the Duchenne boys and a few girls who are the trailblazers for new treatments and research trails. Thank you to Pat Furlong at Parent Project Muscular Dystrophy, you are the first mom who spoke directly to my heart. Thank you to Parent Project Muscular Dystrophy for using the photo of Luke as your 2009 Christmas Card. It's the same picture that I have always wanted to use for this very book. Thank you to my dear "soul" friend Jay Johnson at Healing Life Touch Photography for taking the picture that graces the front cover, the minute I saw it I knew it had to be a book cover. Thank you to Debra Miller founder of CureDuchenne for all your encouragement and believing in me and the Duchenne Movement. Thank you Linda Bjore for pointing out the title "In Your Face" during our getting to know each other session. Knowing the title propelled and inspired me to get to work writing! All the pieces just fell into place. Finally, a great big ball of thank you to Mindy Cameron, without your expert editing skills and your intimate knowledge of Duchenne and pushing me to dig deeper this book transformed into a message of inspiration, action and motivation, the catalyst that propels the Duchenne Movement.

In Love and Transforming Hope Into Action,

Misty

Introduction: Hold On

What would you do if you were told your child would die from a life threatening incurable disease, but before death came your child would require a wheelchair to walk and depend on someone else to provide all their physical needs, that living into adulthood most likely wasn't going to happen? That there isn't anything you can do about it. But, "here take this card and contact the Jerry Lewis Muscular Dystrophy Association."

Would you keel over and die yourself from the pure agony of it, would you go down to the bar and drink your sorrows away? Would you pray like you have never prayed before? Would you convince yourself that "they" are doing everything they can to find a cure? Or, Would it be your "wake up call" to face all and even more than you think you can be?

Further how would you write about something that has ripped your heart out too many times to count at the same time given you a voice of inspiration?

Fasten your seat belt and hold on cause your about to find out.

Chapter One

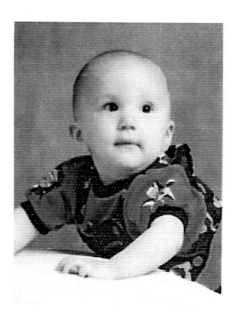

Little Luke (6 months) 1992
Picture taken before we had any idea the word Duchenne even existed, This very year Luke won a beautiful baby contest. I remember thinking how incredible it was to have a beautiful healthy son.

Where's Luke?

L uke was born a healthy bouncing baby boy on December 22 1991. What better gift to receive than a baby for Christmas? Luke's father Pat shed large hot tears that landed on my arm when he first laid eyes on his son. The hospital gave us a giant Christmas stocking to take him home in and I still have the pictures of Luke in the stocking under the Christmas tree.

Now every time I think of Luke's birth I think of the bible verse "Through him you shall know me." For I have come closer than most to the true knowing of the spirit through watching my son face his mortality much sooner than any of us feel comfortable with.

My relationship with Luke's dad was rocky before we married and worsened over time. In a one month time span we were married, miscarried our first child and my dad died. All of these are huge stresses for any relationship, not to mention for kids of only 19. We officially divorced when Luke was two and we have always shared joint physical custody. Luke spends pretty much equal amounts of time at each home. He often says he is the luckiest kid around because he has two parents who love him, two bedrooms, two incredible stepparents, two sisters, two brothers and a family so large that we have to rent the local borough gym for birthday parties.

The first time I had any inkling that there might be something wrong with Luke was when a childcare provider who had special needs children of her own told us that she noticed Luke was not as strong as he should be and that he seemed overly cautious about doing anything physical like the swings or walking up and down stairs. My immediate reaction was anger. "There was nothing wrong with *my* child." I took him to a program called "Child Find" to get him evaluated so that I could prove her wrong. But Luke wouldn't participate in any of the physical tests at all. As I looked around at the other children breezing through the tests, I knew that Luke couldn't perform most of what I as seeing. It was so "In My Face." I can still remember my throat tightening and those first threatening feelings of nausea in the pit of my stomach that would soon become the norm. Somewhere in the back of my mind I knew but I wasn't ready to face it. I quickly pressed the feeling down.

Nagging Feeling

I knew I had to find a doctor and I wanted the very best pediatrician Alaska had to offer. At the time, Alaska's total state population was just over 603,000 and the closest and largest hospital in the state was over an hour and a half away. It was also 1996, just before the internet became the rage that it is today. I had to find a doctor using the old-fashioned Yellow Pages phone book.

The pediatrician I wanted was on vacation but I went ahead and made the appointment anyway. I needed to find out what was going on with my son. More and more "little things" kept taking me back to the same spot. Little things like Luke standing at the top of a long steep staircase crying for my help. This behavior might be normal for a one year old, but definitely not for a 4 year old.

Luke was examined for a long time and pretty soon, every kid doctor on staff at the hospital that day was in the room. I have come to learn over the years that this is never a good sign. They all agreed that Luke was a little small for his age and that he was slower than the average 4 year old. They all said they were pretty sure that he would catch up in a year or two. But just to be on the safe side I was to bring Luke back in year. I, being a young mom with my first child, accepted with relief what I was being told.

Hide-and-Go-Seek

Kids were running all around playing hide-and-go-seek. They were having a blast! When I realized I hadn't seen Luke for some time, I started looking for him. I almost started to panic when I spotted him sitting on a mound of grass. I remember stopping in my tracks and feeling sort of sick inside. He was happy and had a smile on his face but he wasn't participating with the other children. This bothered me big time. I knew something had to be wrong, but I just didn't know what.

Medical Journal

My mom brought over her trusty medical journal with the bad news. The journal described exactly the symptoms my son was having: waddling gait when walking, hard time getting up from the floor, large calf muscles, protruding abdomen. My breath caught in my throat. The sickening feeling in my stomach which was becoming all too familiar, that I had pushed down so many times before, rolled in my gut. I struggled with what I was reading as my mind still wanted to hang onto the idea that everything was fine. After all, my mom was one of 5 sisters who all had healthy boys including my brother. But I knew I had to find out the answers to my burning questions. What was wrong with my little boy? Why wasn't he a monkey? Why didn't he run? Why was he scared to go up and down stairs? Why did he cry and whine all the time?

Mom on a Mission

Enough was enough. I was out for blood by this point. I wasn't going to stop pushing ahead until I found out exactly what was going on with Luke. This time I was going to find the pediatrician I wanted in the first place. I wanted a full blood panel done. I wanted answers.

Dr. Bloodwork (named changed for confidentiality reasons) examined Luke and his face was serious. He not only agreed that we needed to do Luke's blood work, he wanted an additional blood test done to measure the CK or the creatine kinase levels in his blood. If you have extremely elevated CK levels you might have muscular dystrophy.

By the time Luke and I got home a couple of hours later, there was message from Dr. Bloodwork telling us that Luke's dad and I were to come in the next day, which was a Saturday. He also said to make sure that someone else could drive us. No way around it, this was bad news. The message left me barely breathing. I was whirling inside and scared out of my mind! That Friday night was the first of many sleepless nights.

Clown Mobile

I stared at the laughing clown with large curly orange hair swinging from the ceiling, waiting, waiting, waiting. I thought "Damn when was the doctor coming in!" I felt like I was going to vomit. I knew it was bad news, but I was still holding on to the very small hope that everything was fine. When the blow of what the doctor said sunk in, the room started to spin and voices sounded like they were coming from a tunnel. I am not even sure how I walked out of the hospital. I was floating, suffocating, spinning off balance. I remember I felt like I had no legs. I remember Luke's father and my cousin who drove us. I remember feeling relieved that it wasn't my week to have Luke. I couldn't face him yet. How could I? What was I going to do? How was I going to survive?

Family Meeting

I have a very large and local family so I thought it was imperative that I call a family meeting. I wanted to let everyone know about the diagnosis and I only wanted to have to tell the story once. I remember my cousin driving us to the meeting about 30 minutes away. The trees blurred by as we drove. I felt like there was a hurricane of turmoil raging in side of me, threatening to break me in two!

The first person I saw when I walked in was my mother. The other faces were not in focus. As my mother held me up in her arms, the sound that came out of me was a primal call from one mother to the next. The only thing I could say was, "Its bad mamma!" over and over.

My grandma came to stay with me that night and it was a great comfort to have her there with me. I awoke in the middle of the night to her quietly crying out to god. I laid there and listened to her but I was numb. Everything felt like one big nightmare.

Fetal Position

There are no words to describe exactly what the first week of knowing my son had Duchenne Muscular Dystrophy was like. The shock. The grief of lost dreams I once had for my son. I lay in a fetal position for hours on end, weeping, pleading, begging to whom or what I couldn't tell you. I rehashed my situation a million times, always coming to the same outcome. I had to get my life in order. Time to grow up! Time to get past the divorce and time to end relationships that didn't serve me or Luke's highest good. It was high time I pull up the boot straps and love the shit out of my boy! Whatever time I had left with him. I knew it was going to take "ALL" of me. That which does not kill you only makes you stronger, right? Well, I was going to find out.

Light Bulb Question

Sitting at my grandfather's glass kitchen table, feeling numb from head to toe, I was spent from all the crying and grieving, not really knowing which way to go. My Aunt Kendra asked me why I thought this was happening and I said "So I can help other people," as if I had always known the answer. Somehow I knew I had to turn these lemons I had been dealt into something positive, not only for me but for my little boy. The bills had to get paid and life still had to go on. It was up to me now. My life depended on it and Luke depended on it!

Where did this come from

The week after we knew that Luke had Duchenne, my mom, Luke and I all went in to have our genetic blood testing done. Luke needed a formal diagnosis and my mom and I needed to find out if we were carriers. I already knew in my heart that my mother wasn't a carrier and I was. I don't know how I knew, I just knew.

The blood work confirmed is what right: I was a carrier and my mother was not. After the initial wave of guilt washed over me, I felt relieved. I finally knew *why* my boy was different. I was sad because I felt that having more children was out of the question for me and crushed that my boy had a guaranteed struggle ahead of him. Some part of my brain immediately realized that my beloved son would most likely die from Duchenne Muscular Dystrophy.

Chapter Two

Luke Summer 1997
Luke was 5 years old here. He couldn't climb up on the tractor,
Glen had to lift him up there. I love how he seems to be looking
forward to the future and the rest of his life. He looks very happy.

One Foot In Front Of The Other

I felt a deep urgency to provide an excellent quality of life for my son because of the short life expectancy that is part of the Duchenne diagnosis. I refused to look at the negative for long. Somehow I found the strength to immediately take action and I started to read everything I could get my hands on about Duchenne. Even self help books to better myself as a woman and a mother. I got in touch with the Muscular Dystrophy Association and Parent Project Muscular Dystrophy. Every time I faced another issue with the progression of Duchenne I would push back harder and only let myself be overwrought with emotion in bit size pieces. I would dig deep, ask questions and hold fast to the idea of what was actually the best for Luke rather than what the doctors and other people told me to do. I also knew out of every bad thing, good happens. My life was living proof of that.

Something wonderful started to happen almost simultaneously during this early phase of our new life with Duchenne, my personal life took a turn for the better and romance was in the air. I was falling for my good friend Glen, who I think actually fell in love with Luke first. Which led me to moving to one of the most beautiful places in Alaska, VanderWeele Farms, which was owned by Glen's family. It seemed like fate to me because I was actually born in a car parked in the driveway of the main house at VanderWeele Farms some 26 years before!

The farm is a scenic magical place surrounded by magnificent power of the Alaskan mountains and had a way of helping to heal the gaping hole that had been dug into my heart by Duchenne. When I have a bad day all I have to do is look outside or take a walk, breath in and let the peaceful power take over.

I found myself living a life that I hadn't even dreamed of with a man who totally "got" me. I still marvel over the fact that Glen chose a life with Luke and I, knowing full well it was a guaranteed heartache. However I truly believe there are no accidents and that I am meant to be living this life.

Every time I have faced a life-altering event and asked for a sign on what to do I have received it,from what to do about Glen, the birth of my daughter and even Luke. I immediately started Luke on physical therapy but Luke's dad Pat and I decided against steroids. At the time everything I was reading about the long term use of steroids pointed out that steroids would lead to cataracts, diabetes, behavior issues, osteoporosis, cessation of growth, would also stunt puberty and "may" help with longer ambulation and "may" help with respiratory health. This wasn't good enough for me. I felt why give Luke more problems to deal with? Doesn't he have enough problems already? Besides, there was not enough evidence at the time to prove to me that steroids actually helped Duchenne boys walk longer or improved their respiratory function.

Now, 13 years later, there is strong evidence that steroids can help improve some of the symptoms of Duchenne. However for me the use of steroids is a very personal one and only be considered for a quality of life and what is best for your child.

Max

Life had dealt me a huge challenge I knew I had to make a change but I was scared to death for not only Luke's future but my own. The dance steps had been changed but I didn't know the dance. Plus Glen and my relationship was still very new. Even though I wanted to get married. I wanted Glen to be 100% sure that Luke and I were what he wanted. I was not interested in "shaking up" however in lue of my unique situation Glen and I decided we would finish his little farm house he had been building together, enroll Luke into preschool and just see how we managed.

Luke, Glen and I moved in, I started working on the farm and the next natural thing that happened was to get Luke every little boys dream and just about the only thing we could besides love and stability. A puppy seemed a perfect fit. I grabbed at the "normalness". Anything to distance myself from the fact that Luke's childhood wasn't normal or what I had always dreamed of for him. I thought that giving Luke a companion was a great idea.

We picked up the cutest floppy eared puppy with a mask of a husky. Luke decided to name him Max.

Dawn of the TIGER

"ROAR" came a noise out from under the mat that was stood up in the shape of a tent. Our physical therapist, who was in the tent, yelled "NO, DON'T EAT ME!" On all fours, Luke came out roaring like a big tiger and they both laughed and rolled around on the floor. Luke's first experience with physical therapy at the age of 4 was such great fun. I am so thankful for that now. Luke loves physical therapy to this day and actually looks forward to it.

You're Stuck With Us

I think Luke was born a "motor head" with a Hotwheels car in his hand. I would find cars stuffed into every nook and cranny of his car seat and toddler bed. He would wake up with tire imprints on his face. He got his first mini 3 wheeler at the age of 3, then moved on to a 4-wheeler and rode it until he couldn't physically get on the thing.

By the time he was 4, Luke could tell you the make of every vehicle that was on the road without ever getting one wrong. That's probably the real reason my Glen, a motor head himself, fell in love with Luke, but don't tell him I told you that. The three of us were heading down the road, playing the Chevy, Ford, Dodge, Toyota game when Luke told Glen that he was *stuck* with us. Glen looked at me and said that was all right by him. That was the moment that I knew Glen was my man.

You Are My Sunshine

Luke and I went from sharing the same bedroom for 3 years to him having his very own "Big Boy" room when we moved in with Glen. Luke was only five and the night separation from me was a very hard transition for him to make. I would put him in bed and then the screaming and crying would start. Luke would cry "I don't want to go to bed" or "I need a drink of water" or "I need to go pee." He would work himself up into a frenzy of a sweating frightened boy. After yelling at him, pleading with him and trying to ignore him, I would get up and go into his room and hold him and sing his favorite song, "You Are My Sunshine." He would settle down but the minute I walked out, he would start in again. Glen and I would lay in bed at a loss for what to do for him. A few weeks into the behavior he started hollering, "Mommy save me!" It was so heartbreaking and I would say "Yes Luke, I will save you." Later Luke's plea turned into a simple request of "Save me." This ripped my heart out!

These night fits lasted for months. I was pretty sure he didn't understand about Duchenne and that he was just trying to get attention. I was at my wit's end with it until one night I wasn't going to take it anymore. I grabbed the "Happy Spoon" and the kitchen timer and walked into his room, looked him in the eye and stated, "I am going to set the timer for 15 minutes, so cry, kick, scream, do whatever you want for 15 minutes, but when this timer goes off, I want silence! "If you continue to scream I am going to spank your ass!" Luke was immediately silent and he laid quietly until the timer went off. Then he said "Mom the timer went off." We never had a problem again. The episodes were over just like that.

Gene Therapy Trials

On the crisp sunny September morning that Luke started Kindergarten I was a mix of emotions. My little boy was starting school and he wouldn't be with me with for several hours a day. What would happen if he fell? Or the teacher wasn't there for him? I had met Luke's teacher already and thought he was a very nice teddy bear of a man. He seemed like the perfect match for Luke but even this did nothing to ease my nerves.

After dropping Luke off I went to the post office to pick up our mail. There was a letter from some organization, I think it must have been the Muscular Dystrophy Association, notifying me that Luke was eligible to enter the all new "Gene Therapy Trials." I sent in Luke's application that very same day. I felt to have this news only a year after diagnosis was a sign that a cure was close.

I shared the gene therapy news with Luke's teacher and that evening he called me and asked if it would be okay for the kindergarten class to paint pictures to sell at an Art Show to help fund Luke going to the trials. I told him that Luke hadn't been picked yet, but he insisted, saying that it didn't matter and that he wanted to do this for Luke.

A few weeks later, the little masterpieces that the students painted were put on pretty water colored white cardboard and plastic wrapped. Each painting unique, each painting for Luke. Humbled and deeply touched, this was first time I felt in awe that someone did something so incredibly wonderful for Luke in the hope that he would be saved.

We found out shortly thereafter that Luke hadn't been picked for the trials. Outwardly I resonated hope and positivity, but inwardly I was crushed. The roller coaster continued as we went on living day to day.

On a Wing and a Prayer

When the MDA approached me about having Luke as their poster child for the Alaska chapter, we jumped at the chance. I had always had a bittersweet realization that I could help other people through my personal journey with Luke and DMD.

In September of 1998, Alaska Parenting Magazine journalist Kristen Seine wrote an article about Luke and I called "On a Wing and a Prayer: A 5-Year-Old Fights a Deadly Disease." The table of contents caption read "A mother and son fight a deadly disease with faith, hope and a positive outlook." When I saw Luke's face on the front cover all I could do was cry! This only happened to other people. Not to me. I wanted so desperately to change places with someone else. There it was again. The excruciating pain that lingers below the surface every minute of every day. An agony that never totally subsides. Luke was quoted in the article saying" I can't wait to when I can run!"

The article later won the National Parenting Publications Award, Seine said "I'm really honored that we won a national award for this story about Luke and his mother. Meeting them had a profound impact on me because their courage and positive outlook must take incredible strength. I am glad someone else was touched by their story, too."

Good Will Ambassador

Luke served as the Muscular Dystrophy Association's Goodwill Ambassador for Alaska from 1999 until 2001. Luke loved the attention and he was pampered and given gifts at every Fill The Boot Campaign or Lock Up event that we attended. But all that attention had a huge drawback when he started to expect the same treatment at home. When I asked him one day to put up his clothes, he didn't want to and said "You can't make me. You know what I have!" I instantly replied "I of all people KNOW what you have and you will not use it as a crutch to get your way! You put your clothes away right now while you still can." I then called the MDA and told them that Luke would only be doing a few appearances until he had a better attitude. I feel that kids need to be a part of the family and help out with the household chores. I also felt Luke needed to do things for himself while he still had the ability. I have never wavered from this belief.

Long Way Home

The summer had been great with working on the farm, playing with Luke and back yard barbeques. But when October came around I hadn't been feeling well. I seemed to be tired all the time and my period was a few days late. I thought I'd go to the doctor to see if I was anemic since I had had trouble with low iron levels before.

When the doctor told me I was pregnant I looked at her in shock and disbelief. Here I was in a serious relationship but not yet married, my son had muscular dystrophy and I had a 50-50 chance of having another affected child. This was not news that I was ready to hear. Before I headed home from the doctor's office to tell Glen the news, I took the long way home in an effort to get my head on straight. I had to be absolutely sure what I was going to do no matter what Glen decided or wanted. I felt that if we were going to have a child, we were going to do it happily and on purpose knowing full well what we were up against. After all *every* life is miraculous!

Glen was sitting on the couch and I was sitting on the floor, crying with my back against the couch, my legs stretched out under the coffee table. I can't remember the exact words I used to tell Glen he was going to be a daddy, but I do remember how quiet he was, how unreadable he was. I remember being so worried about what was going on in his mind. I told him that I understood if having a child wasn't what he wanted but that I intended on having the baby with or without him. I said that if he chose to be with me and the baby, we would both have to agree on it happily. And of course, we talked about the possibility of having a child with Duchenne together.

Glen broke his silence by saying we were having a girl. I said, "We?" and he said, "Yes cause we were going to get married!" I said, "No we aren't, you haven't asked me yet." He jumped up and ran to the phone and called my dear friend Donna the wedding coordinator and asked her if she would go ring shopping with him. He then proceeded to make several calls, all to family, telling them, "We are pregnant and getting married!"

We decided on a January wedding because I'd be only 4 months along and not showing too much. I put my boys in matching tuxedos with tails. Glen told Luke the tails were "mud flaps". I'll never figure out boys and their fascination with car parts.

Now that I had told Glen, Luke was next. I was pretty sure he would be more than okay with having a sibling, possibly even excited. I was right. He was only 8 years old and he'd never been around anyone that was pregnant before. I don't think he really understood what was happening until I started to show. The baby would get hiccups all the time and Luke thought that was pretty cool. He would put his little hand on my tummy to feel the hiccups. He loved watching my tummy "bump up" as he called it.

On July 11, 1999, our baby girl Jenna was born two weeks early. I nearly died from a pulmonary embolism after giving birth and was in pretty bad shape but she was perfect. I called her Pumpkin, daddy called her Turnip, and Luke fondly called her Pickle. She was so cute and she completed our family. Luke immediately took on the big brother role with pride. Now Luke had a sister to love and to be love.

Chapter Three

Luke and Puppy Max 1998
Luke was having a hard time walking through the snow, especially with heavy winter boots. He wanted so bad to be able to run with his dog. So I put him in the sled and I would run while pulling him so Max could run with Luke.

I Can Heal My Life

I n Chapter two I mentioned I found myself living a life I had "never" dreamed, with an incredible chance at a life of my choice. I never dreamed I would have to face the probable human outcome of my own child dieing before me much less finding the love of my life. Here I was madly in love with Glen and our home spun farm lifestyle while trying with all my might to focus on the positive, not my son dieing. I knew I had to dig to the depths of my soul with courage to find a braveness I wasn't sure I even had. When I was a kid average was viewed as okay because at least that meant I was passing and not being a problem. You could say I was not taught how to be the best me or to even love myself. But I knew I had to figure it out. If to non other than to not be debilitated by grief I felt for Luke, not to mention I was a wife to an incredible guy and I was a mother of not just one child but two. They depend on me. A friend of mine at the time suggested I read a book titled "You Can Heal Your Life by Louise Hay. I completely resonated with the fact that the point of power is now, the present moment and that thoughts are all we are ever dealing with at any given time, with the best part being able to change our thoughts! The book also brought to my attention we must nurture the body, mind and spirit as one. HMMM, you mean I could choose what I am thinking about Luke's disease and that I am not a bad person being punished after all, that I could choose to rise above to live life with courage and triumph? That I could actually love and give myself all that I need? My soul soaked up this new information like a sponge. I wanted to live like this, I wanted to raise Luke and Jenna with this knowledge, which I have, but also at the time I had this idea since my son and I had been dealt a "Bad Hand" no more bad things would ever happen again, life would run smoothly and everyone would understand. This was also the time I figured out that there are 3 kinds of people in this world. First kind are the angles who truly care, wanting to help and make a difference...they totally "get" you and your current situation.

Second are the one's who mean well and say the understand but really don't. These are the kind that can be he most challenging and third...my favorite which I write with clenched teeth are the kind that really don't give a damn, the heck with you and the outcome as long as they get their job done...GRRRR!!! All issues that have come up over the years have had elements of ease and elements of great anguish and pain the two later kinds of people always the crux of the matter.

Wheel Barrel

Luke went from liking school to not wanting to go. Come to find out he was having troubles in P.E. Class. Luke was 7 at the time. I called up the MS. PE to see if I could find out what was going on, I asked her if she had read Luke's file. And she said she had and invited me in to one of her classes with Luke. All the kids were broken up in partners. Luke and I were paired as well. There were stations set up around the gym, we came to the wheel barrel station. You know were one partner holds up the legs of the other so they can walk using just their arms. Luke had never been able to hold up his own weight with just his arms, so he started to cry. MS P.E. says to Luke...come on Luke show your mom you can do it. I have seen you do it before. My mind screamed, What! I was so frustrated and hurt. One because the P.E. teacher obviously did not understand and two Luke, my little boy did not have the strength to do the wheel barrel and three I was not sure how to fix the problem. I waited for the teacher after school to speak with her. I was around 6 months pregnant and very emotional. MS. PE looked down at my tummy and said I think we should talk about this when you are less emotional. Are you kidding me?? To make a long story short I ended up putting Luke in adaptive P.E. Hence the problem was fixed.

MS. Sped Bus

I was laying in the hospital bed after just delivering my daughter which almost cost me my life. Luke was suppose to start summer school were he would also get his physical therapy done when I got a call from my grandmother who was watching Luke that the bus did not show up to take Luke to school. I immediately call the special ed busing department at our local school bus barn to find out why because they had picked him up the previous week from his dads house. MS. Sped Bus informed me that she did not feel that it was right for joint shared custody parents to make the bus come to both houses. I said, so that is your opinion. My tax dollars help pay busing so what was the difference? She said well we just can't pick him up at both houses. Had to get student support services involved in that one.

Bath Tub Fun

At the time we had a HUGE bright lipstick red bathtub...I loved to fill it up with bubbles and have crazy fun with the kids. I had gotten in the habit of taking pictures. This was right before digital cameras became the rage. I go went and picked up the photos. I remember I coulnd't wait to look at them. I ripped open the envelope. I flipped through the pictures I suddenly stopped. There in the tub was my chubby little 8month old baby girl and the skinniest, sickliest bony kid stared smiling back at me. He looked like a holocaust victim. Tears sprang to my eyes and I ran all the way to the car. I vomited and sobbed. Flashing before my eyes was the death of Luke. I had this deep sense Luke wouldn't live past his 14th birthday! I called my in home support person Gwen. She came over immediately and I had the first of two complete mental break downs since Luke's diagnosis

The Luke Sled

Glen is a builder and inventor by instinct. He can turn a picture into reality. He lives for making life easier for others. He is also very very good at surprises and keeping them secret. The sled he built for Luke to pull behind the snowmobile was no different. Luke could no longer ride in front of us when we would go snowmobiling because he was getting too tall and was losing upper body strength at such an alarming rate that he could no longer stop himself from falling forward. Glen knew that we needed a suitable and safe way for Luke to still enjoy riding with us.

One day I came home to find a sled with a roll bar, lights and seat belt that Luke could operate on his own. The paint Glen chose was perfectly fitting for life on a farm that depends on John Deere Tractors: John Deere green and yellow with an old John Deere mud flap hanging from the back. Painted on the side was the name "Luke". Even though the sled was for Luke, it was like Glen had made the sled for me. Glen had figured out early on how to touch my heart and that was through Luke. It is called love.

Give me 5 + 1

I am the oldest of 2 other siblings, my brother, Boone 4 years younger and my sister Autumn is 19 years younger, mom was having her as I was leaving home. Then coming into the VanderWeele family brought me Glen's sister and brother and their spouses.

Over a period of six years I had been blessed with not one, but 5 nephews! My Brother having a son first, then my sister in law with 2 boys, plus one girl, my favorite niece so far, I am still holding out for my brother and sister who is 21 for more nieces. As well as my brother in law with 2 boys.

I am completely in awe of them and thrilled that I can watch them in their cute little sports uniforms running and playing like boys should. Additionally, I feel that at least Luke can experience sports through them. As I have said, my son has always been a motor head without much interest in sports except for Nascar! He loves his cousins and appreciates that they are all healthy and don't have the stress of weakening muscles. He doesn't begrudge them for having a normal childhood. Luke and I both feel extremely honored and thankful for each and every one of them.

When Luke was diagnosed my brother was 22. I am not sure what his reaction was but over the years I know he has felt very sorry for what I am going through but has told me in his very heart felt way that I am his hero. And my beautiful "little" sister who I have been connected to since in the womb was only 9. She has always been Luke and my number one fan. The some 19 years age difference many time has put me in the mother roll, but now that she is getting older it is more of a sister sister roll. She is the person who is my shoulder more times than I can count. I also know it kills her inside to have to watch Luke's body deteriorate and I know her heart goes out to me continually.

Grandma with the white Chevy truck

"God willing and the creeks don't rise," was one of my grandmother's favorite sayings. It was her way of saying anything can happen. She always drove a four wheel drive truck and she took me hiking as a little girl and we would skinny dip in the mountain lakes. Together we would go for ice cream in our jammies at 2 am and she was always taking photos when you least expected it. She was my rock when I needed her and she was my number one fan and Luke's best friend until the day she passed. He fondly called her "grandma with the white Chevy truck."

She died in my arms with one last smile and a tear just for me. Although I was sad about her death, I was glad she wasn't in pain from her lung cancer any longer. Her entire memorial service was dedicated to Luke. The minister read words she wrote at her celebration of life. She wrote: "Do not be afraid when it is your time to pass over to heaven. I'll be waiting, ready to hold your hand." I can just envision her with glowing light radiating from her. She went from being my rock to being Luke's guardian angel.

Chapter Four

Santa Luke 2002 Ms. McNiven 3rd Grade
The progression of Duchenne starting to take it toll. Luke could still walk a bit, only used the wheelchair at school or long trips.

Freedom

I f I tried hard enough I could go for days, some times even a couple months cursing along like everything was normal until I would drive by a soccer field or watch Luke get up from the floor when overwhelming anguish and fear would send me downward, reeling and grieving. At these times I would go rent a sad movie, turn off the phone and grab the box of tissues and hide until I felt better.

It was a strange kind of surreal time. I had one child losing independence and another gaining it. I was ultra sensitive to the internal tug-of-war that I felt inside between happiness and sadness. I was buying new walking shoes, ice skates and jump ropes for one child and leg braces and wheelchairs for the other. The dreaded idea of having to put Luke in a wheelchair was becoming a reality. In my mind it made Duchenne more real, more devastating. I wondered and feared what Luke would think and how family and others would react. Would kids pick on him? How would we get the wheelchair into our home? Was it time? How old were Duchenne boys normally put into a wheelchair? I remember thinking that God picked the wrong person for the job. The stress I felt was often times insurmountable. However I always ended right back to the thought that it was how I was thinking about what was happening that was causing such stress. So if I could flip my thoughts to more positive I could not feel as much pain. I would have this chat with myself, "okay Misty, you got a choice here, stay miserable or ask to be shown the way.”

Besides Glen and his family at my side, I had very little support from my immediate family. I don't think they knew how to support me and so it was easier to pretend that none of it was happening. My mom tried and would babysit the kids from time to time, but I could tell that she was having a hard time with it, especially Luke's physical decline.

Call From The School Nurse

The decision to order the wheelchair came after a horrible incident at school. I received a phone call from the school nurse saying that there had been an accident and that I should come and get Luke, who she said was OK but shaken up. She then told me that Luke had been trampled by another class that was headed out to recess. Have you ever had one of those calls where you just can't believe what the person on the other end is saying? This was one of those kinds of calls.

I tried to keep my car under the speed limit as I shot over to the school. The sting of tears was blinding me and my heart was breaking. I bounced from feeling anger greater than I had ever felt to a burning exploding urgency that I can only describe as a primal instinct to protect my child. How could any of this be happening to my sweet boy? That day I knew it was time for a wheelchair.

When I got to school I learned that the class that trampled Luke had a substitute teacher who was unaware of the situation. This did little to make me feel better, as I think Luke's physical weakness should be mentioned to every member of staff and anyone else working at the school. The minute I laid eyes on Luke, I knew that he was upset. I hugged him tight but said nothing as I needed to calm down.

Later that night I held him close and told him I was sorry for what had happened and I asked him what he thought about having a wheelchair to use at school. He was apprehensive but thought it would be great to try.

Blessing in Disguise

We had decided that the wheelchair would be used only at school until Luke needed it more. This would ensure that he wouldn't fall or be trampled. Although that gave some relief, it didn't change the fact that DMD was ever present in Luke's little body.

Every step down the path of DMD's progression meant one step nearer to death. Still in my face no matter what I did.

The day the wheelchair was dropped off I silently wept until I saw Luke's face. This new contraption had the one thing that Luke loved most: WHEELS! Luke's smile lit up the entire school gym. His excitement was so obvious, like a teenager over their first car. Finally Luke could feel the wind in his face as he raced down the hallway or across the parking lot. For once Luke could feel freedom and mobility for himself, all by himself. The wheelchair was a blessing in disguise and it gave Luke a huge esteem boost. You could see and feel the relief he felt to finally feel safe.

Luke took off like a pro, like he had been driving his entire life! Glen told him to keep his mouth closed as to not get bugs stuck in his teeth. Later we took Luke over to the farm to show Glen's parents. We loaded the wheelchair into the back of Glen's truck because we didn't have a van yet. Glen told his dad Ben how heavy the little Junior Model electric wheelchair was but Ben was having none of it. He said "Oh no, how much could that thing weigh?" and dared Luke to drive over his foot. Luke looked at him to make sure it was okay and then drove over Ben's foot. Ben never asked Luke to drive over his foot again.

A few months later we bought a minivan and suitcase ramp so we could haul Luke and his wheelchair around. Luke was still walking a bit, but it was sure nice to be able to take Luke places without worrying about him falling or getting too tired.

The wheelchair did bring one new problem. How in the heck were we to get it into our house? I contacted our in-home support person Gwen and she found a one-time Alaska Housing grant available for disability home modifications. The grant was just enough to cover the cost of building a ramp for a two story home.

Now the only problem was having a wheelchair and a crawling baby in the same house. Luke was extra careful not to run over his baby sister. Then as she began to walk she would stand and hold onto the back and Luke would give her rides. She loved it!

Cherish These Days

Instinctively I reached for both of my children, Jenna 8 months, Luke almost 9, and the life I was creating with Glen. I decided to cherish each and every minute, every precious moment. I wanted to live life to the fullest and with as much purpose as I could muster. So when the phone call came in from The Make-A-Wish Foundation, an organization that grants "wishes" to children with life threatening medical conditions, I took it as a sign that I was on the right track. But that call also hit me like a big wave of reality because only kids that are going to die get "wishes." Death was yet again in my face.

Luke originally wanted to go to Hawaii, but the foundation said it would be hard to find activities for Luke to do for an entire week. His second choice was Disney World in Florida. Jenna was only 8 months old so we decided that she would not go with us. What a trip it was with me and my new husband and Luke's dad and his girlfriend! It doesn't sound very traditional, but boy was it a blast for all of us! Luke took turns sleeping in each parents' room, so the couples could go out for grownup fun every other night.

By this point my relationship with Pat was calm and reserved as we had been divorced nearly 6 years. That's plenty of time for the waters to settle. We both want what is best for Luke and somehow we seem to push our thoughts, feelings and the past aside. I guess we were never a very good match as our personalities are completely different. Pat is quiet and hard to read while I am a spitfire full of chaotic energy. I need to have several things on the fire at once and I like decisions to be made quickly. I don't understand others who sit on the fence or don't show their feelings.

I have some sad memories of that trip too and looking back, I suppose I was a mess in the lead up to it. I had so much on my mind that when we got to Disney World, I discovered that I had left my purse on the plane with all of my money, my identification, and my cell phone in it. I never got any of it back.

Even walking the streets of Disney and hearing all the music triggered a deep sense of nostalgia and heart wrenching pain. Luke's delighted smile had me wondering how many more years I would have with him. Would it kill me to lose him? What about my daughter?

I was a bit of a confused mess, trying to be fun, organized and happy for Luke while I was dying inside. I had a lot of conversations with myself about the importance of pulling it together, to bite the bullet and go on. My choices were either wallow in self pity or grab the reins and look for the positive.

Here Come's Santa Claus

Grade school Christmas programs are every parent's' delight, seeing children with their goofy little smiles and cute little bodies singing "Here Come Santa Claus" a little off key. It was Luke's second Christmas with his wheelchair and the teacher thought it would be a great idea to have Luke play Santa Claus with 8 classmates as reindeer. Luke was the cutest, skinniest little kid in a red Santa suit that I had ever seen. He wore painted on red cheeks and a Santa hat, held the reins of his reindeer, and shouted "HO, HO, HO!" It was a wonderful sight through my tears of joy. Luke was included as a "normal" kid. The teacher just smiled and as I teared up so did other parents. Everyone was clapping.

Luke's grade school years were filled with tons of support from teachers and Luke's physical therapists. There were several of us parents with "special kids" and we bonded close together. Even one of Luke's teachers had a blind son. This made for an accepting environment which I am very grateful for because middle school was an entirely different matter all together.

Human Pancake

When Luke was 11, his 3-year-old sister Jenna was a bundle of energy. Luke's wheelchair enabled him to keep up with his little sister and he would race along behind her as she ran as fast as she could. Luke would yell "I'm gonna get you!" and the two of them would laugh and laugh.

Well, electric wheelchairs have this feature that makes them automatically stop on a dime if the driver lets up on the joystick. Luke could really gather up some speed in our big house and one day, he let off the joystick too soon and went flying face first onto the floor. SMACK! His front tooth nearly pierced the skin of his lip. As I raced to help him, my soul was screaming and all I could do was cry with him as he lay there bleeding, unable to get himself up. That was the day that Luke started wearing a seatbelt.

Shiny Penny

The Muscular Dystrophy Association provides a yearly "Summer Camp" where kids with MD can go for a week and feel like normal kids that fit in with everyone else. For Luke, camp has always been a highlight of the summer. The year that stands out most in my mind is the year that I brought my mother-in-law with me to drop off Luke.

I have always gone with a more holistic approach to Luke's healthcare and I am proud of the level of care that he receives. Every summer he spends many many hours outside in the sun and by August, he sports a pretty good tan. If it weren't for his wheelchair, he would look like a vision of good health. He doesn't take regular medications and he looks like any other teen, complete with a touch of acne. When we went over to the nurses station to drop off Luke's liquid vitamins and Probiotics, I noticed the HUGE pile of medicines dropped off by other parents for their kids. I wondered just how many of those medications were truly necessary? I looked around and saw so many overweight kids with sickly faces that I almost felt guilty that Luke was so healthy. As we drove away I glanced over at my mother-in-law and saw tears in her eyes. She said, "Luke looks so good." I said "I know, he looks like a shiny penny compared to those other kids" and we just cried together. She told me that I was doing a great job with him.

Alaskan Outdoor Fun

While MDA summer camp is the highlight of Luke's summer, what we do every March is the highlight of the winter. We pack up everything we own, put the snowmobiles, sleds and gear on a trailer and head north up the Parks Highway to the Cottini's Larson Lake Lodge about 100 miles away. Bonnie and Pio schedule a weekend every winter just for Luke to come out and ice fish, visit and "kick'it" out on the deck. They always provide a memorable time, from fireworks to the outdoor hot tub to watching the stars at night.

Oh,and did I mention that the cabins don't have running water or electricity and there's no road to get there? The only way you can get there in the winter is by snowmobile, dog sled or airplane. A few can make it by cross country skiing or mountain biking, but that's clearly not an option for a family that includes a wheelchair. For us, going by snowmobile is by far the easiest way. But easy is a relative term when you consider that we have to take Luke's 500 pound power wheelchair, his manual wheelchair, his bed, and his bi-pap and cough assist machines out there.

Once there we have to take care of Luke's needs, like going to the bathroom, cold weather protection and sleeping. Over the years we have put our minds to the task and have come up with some pretty cool ideas to make it all happen and give Luke a family fun winter vacation.

For me, going to 'the cabin' as we call it, puts Luke's progression of Duchenne right up close in my face with nowhere to run. At home, modern conveniences and my daily routines make things easier and take my mind off the fact that DMD is ravaging Luke's body at a very sickening and alarming rate. But at the cabin, it is all so "In Your Face!" It's hard enough taking care of him at home, but doing it in a place where there is no indoor plumbing or electricity takes it to a whole new level for everyone in the family. Emotionally it is always a challenge and one year, I had my second DMD induced mental breakdown. I locked myself in the bathroom and cried like I have never cried before, overwhelmed with agony and joy at the same time.

There are times when I feel like I'm the wrong person for this job. That the pain is just too much. Then something or someone comes along and reminds me it is so much easier to be happy. It always strikes me how humbled I feel for having friends like the Cottini's wanting to give Luke and our family some winter fun. Everyone needs friends like them.

Close Call

It was fall and the leaves were turning a little bit yellow and orange. The sun was out sparkling through the trees. The day was beautiful and good. I was a chaperone for a group of third graders on a school field trip based on lessons about salmon and their migration from the ocean to Alaska's streams, creeks, lakes and rivers. The Department of Fish and Game were stocking salmon in a nearby local lake and around the lake is a smooth enough trail for Luke to drive his wheelchair. At one end of the lake the water is so deep that you can't see the bottom. The section of trail around this end has a steep wooded embankment on one side. Luke was about 10 feet in front of me when I turned around to check on the other kids. As I turned, I saw Luke's wheelchair out of the corner of my eye. It was lurching forward and headed straight down the embankment toward the lake! As I took off after him, I focused on keeping his limbs from being mangled as the wheelchair flipped over and slid downward. I put everything I had into stopping the wheelchair and unclipping Luke's seatbelt, for I knew that if he went in, he would be trapped underwater. Somehow I was able to get to him before he went in. It was as if some big helping hand came down and all 350 pounds of boy and wheelchair came to a halt about half way down the embankment.

Neither one of us had a scratch on us, which was a miracle in itself because I was wearing shorts. Two dads who were also chaperoning came running and they were able to bring Luke and his wheelchair up to the trail. Later the kids told me that I literally flew down the hill after Luke like I had wings or something. The next day my entire body hurt like I had been hit by a Mack truck. Luke told me on the way home that day that he felt grandma was there. I told him that his guardian angel is always with him and that she was doing a pretty darn good job! Luke agreed.

Fifth Grade Field Trip

In celebration and farewell to Middle School every year the 5th graders head down to Homer, a small Alaska Coastal City located on Kachemak Bay, for adventure, "tide pooling" and learning about Alaskan sea life. The kids look forward to this three day field trip all winter.

Luke's teacher, Mr Lytle, had made the trip the year before with Luke's friend Steven, who had Duchenne as well. It was decided that me and another parent, a father whose boy Tommy is blind, would go along on the trip since our boys needed extra help. Tommy's dad would be better at helping with Luke's physical needs and so we thought it would work better if he acted as Luke's legs and I acted as Tommy's eyes. I was happy with this because you can imagine how hard it is to push a manual wheelchair through sand and rocks. Our arrangement worked out very well and was extra special since Luke and Tommy were good friends.

This trip was a challenge for me. I usually keep myself busy by focusing on Luke's needs and my daily routine but now I watched someone else do everything that needs doing for my boy. I forced myself to stay focused because I had to help Tommy navigate the beach terrain but I couldn't help but worry about all of the physical work that Tommy's dad was doing for Luke. There were many times when Luke's teacher would grab the front of the wheelchair and Tommy's dad would grab the back and they could carry Luke down the beach to all of the action happening at the tide pools. I felt torn. On one hand, what an incredible sight to have two grown men helping and caring for Luke and on the other hand, there was Duchenne glaring at me.

Luke was also taking his own frustration about his lack of mobility out on me. I am sure that being a pre-teen didn't help matters much. During dinners back at the school where we were staying, Luke would sit with his friends and tell me to sit somewhere else even though he needed my help to eat. Luke had never treated me like this before. All I wanted to do was run and hide. I was embarrassed that Luke was treating me this way but at the same time, I was devastated that Luke required so much assistance. It was apparent that Luke didn't like it either.

Chapter Five

**Jenna, Misty, Glen and Luke Before Back Surgery 2005
Luke was so used to his body he didn't realize how slumped over
and uncomfortable he was or even that his feet were curling in
from lack of use and muscle deterioration.**

Every Life is Precious

By this stage of the journey, despite the consuming pain of watching Luke deteriorate physically, the beauty that shows through in life, like the flower growing between the cracks of the sidewalk or the mother holding hands with her child as they cross the road, was all around me and ever present. I just had to look. You see every life is precious from the moment of conception to the day we die. No one knows when it's their time to pass. It could be today, it could be tomorrow, but we will all pass over. It is a guarantee.

But sometimes it did feel like time was moving too quickly. Luke was walking less and less and I worried about how I was going to be able to take care of him. I felt very strongly that it wasn't Luke's stepdad's ultimate responsibility to provide what Luke needed. I really didn't know what I was doing but with the help of my in-home support person, Gwen, I literally went on a mission to find out what I needed to do to provide for Luke's increasing needs. I found several grants for medical equipment and modifying our bath room and our 80 foot of ramp so Luke could get into the house. I also jumped right in to special needs workshops, learning everything I needed to know about advocating, day to day care and the school system.

Time went on and I was able to get everything that Luke needed and at the same time start my own business. Looking back I see that I was keeping myself extra busy with life so the pain didn't seem so real. That just maybe there would either be a cure or Luke would pass so the madness would end.

Middle school is often a tough time for any pre-teen but even more so for a middle school boy in a wheelchair. Luke was bored and we were having trouble with his behavior. He would lash out at his aides, his teachers, and even at me. Luke later shared with me that he felt like he was cursed and that he was very frustrated with life at the time. He remembers one teacher telling his aide to go to the office while she locked the door and put Luke's wheelchair in manual mode so he couldn't go anywhere. That's the equivalent of holding someone down and not letting them get up. We fondly call this teacher "Fairy Godmother from Shrek 2": the hair, the glasses, the sweet and nice person on the outside hiding the mean and unhappy person on the inside.

Those three years of middle school were full of dreadful hard times that attacked me and challenged me on every level. Physically, Luke was getting bigger and it was hard on me to always be picking him up. Mentally it seemed a challenge with every teacher. Duchenne Muscular Dystrophy was ravaging my boy's body with a vengeance: he was starting to slump over from scoliosis and that in turn put pressure on his bowels, lungs and internal organs. I wondered when it was going to end and spiritually, I was beginning to wonder about the real meaning of life. We were being forced to make hard and life-altering medical decisions which would impact Luke and the entire family for the rest of our lives. I also worried that Luke's dad might be a challenge as it was evident that he was having a hard time accepting Luke's Duchenne. I also had to consider the emotional well being of my daughter who was starting to worry about her brother.

Brother and Sister

There are nearly 8 years between Luke and Jenna so it wouldn't seem that they would be close but this isn't the case. Sure, they have their sibling quarrels and are sometimes jealous of each other but their bond has always been strong. From the day that Jenna was born, Luke has been very much the overprotective big brother. I took him with us when Jenna needed shots as a baby and when she would cry, Luke would be furious at the nurse for hurting her. As Jenna has gotten older her protectiveness and awareness of Luke and his medical condition have only proven to strengthen their relationship.

When Luke started using his wheelchair and could no longer get up from the floor, Glen bought a pre-made laminate countertop and put legs on it, making it the perfect height for Luke and his wheelchair. Jenna sits on a bar stool on one side and Luke on the other and this small invention has enabled them to play with each other. During the early years, the play was pretty much all imaginary and board games.

Now the "Big Table" is Lego Nation and is used mostly for building things. Luke and Jenna have figured out how to satisfy the 10-year-old engineer in Jenna while promoting Luke's ingenuity. And let's face it, at 18 Luke has little interest in pretend play.

Another one of my favorite things to watch is when they tie a wagon to Luke's wheelchair in the summer or a sled in the winter and he pulls Jenna around. She screams and throws her hands up in a gesture like it is the fastest ride she has ever been on!

Hand Bell Hell

Remember when I told you that there are three kinds of people in this world and that the people who say they understand but really don't can cause the most frustration? Well this is what Luke being in the hand bell choir was like. Luke could still hold the light hand bells and play small segments of the music and his teacher, Mr. Music, said he was working out a way for Luke to continue to play. Although he may have tried, in the end Mr. Music could not put his desire for perfection aside in order to help give Luke some much needed self esteem. He insisted that Luke play music that was much too hard for him physically and then he vented his frustration out at him. I simply could not understand this man's reasoning and attitude and when the situation became untenable, I felt I had no choice but to take Luke out of the class. It was a hard lesson for me because I have always believed that you have to follow through with your commitments and Luke had made a commitment to the hand bell choir. But DMD makes you change many of your long held beliefs and this was just another example of that.

Stephanie

The phone call came in the morning on the day after the Fourth of July. My friend Tesa's 19-year-old daughter Stephanie had been killed in a freak car accident. I rushed to the funeral home to meet Tesa and her husband. I sat with her when the funeral director told her it would not be a good idea for her to see her daughter's body. I watched her pick out the urn and make all the funeral arrangements. My heart ached for her. About a year later while talking on the phone, Tesa told me she didn't know how I did it. She said what I was going through with Luke was harder than losing her Stephanie. I said "No Way! At least I still have Luke with me." I was shocked that she considered my pain worse! Isn't pain pain? She has to live each day without ever seeing her daughter again, and I have to live each day waiting for the other shoe to drop while watching muscle weakness take over Luke's body. But Luke is still very much alive and I cherish each day with him.

Before Stephanie's death I had always thought that losing a child would kill you. I couldn't see how a parent could go on. Watching Tesa and her family go on has been enlightening. They have proven to me that life goes on. That you can treasure this life and the many gifts and little miracles that make it worth living. Life is meant to be lived full on!

Lesson in Water Safety

My aunt had a big family party to celebrate the July 4th holiday at her lake house. All of us were having a ball barbequeing, swimming and jet skiing. Luke was 11 and was already on his second wheelchair after growing out of the first cute little junior model. He drove down to the water's edge where my brother was about to take 3 or 4 little cousins out for a ride on jet ski and so we put Luke in a life jacket a little too big for him, tied it tight and put him on the jet ski in the front of my brother. They made several trips back and forth in front of the beach. Things got a little rowdy out there with all of the kids tipping the thing from side to side. It went over a little bit too far and it turned onto its side, throwing everyone into the water. Luke and my brother landed on the side facing away from the beach so we could not see what was going on. My brother frantically yelled "HELP!" and my cousin tore off his shirt and dove in to assist. A ouple of others grabbed the canoe. I stood there not at all worried at first, until it dawned on me that my brother was having a hard time keeping both himself and Luke above water. I waited silently. I felt if I moved something worse would happen.

They came ashore and my brother told me he was sorry and I hugged him. He then told us what had happened: My brother was wearing blue jeans and they got so heavy when he went into the water that he could barely swim. Then Luke slipped through his life jacket! These two factors almost cost someone's life! A very big lesson. A) always wear a life jacket and B) always wear a life jacket.

After the lake incident my brother seemed unsure of how to handle Luke. I think it scared him so much that he now keeps his distance. I know he loves Luke and me dearly but that was just too close of a call for him.

Secret Christmas Project

"The Greatest Stepdad on Earth" is what Luke calls Glen. One of Glen's gifts is a natural talent for making things and he can fix anything almost blindfolded. He takes great pride in being able to make life easier for Luke and he has enabled Luke to have life experiences that would not have been possible without his resourcefulness and ingenuity. Needless to say, all of this makes me love him that much more.

During one Christmas season, my sister Autumn, who was 15 at the time, was living with us and doing a secret project with Glen. On many occasions she would show up with red paint on her clothes wearing a big smile. Glen would just walk by smiling that smile that says he has a secret and he isn't going to share it.

On Christmas morning Glen got up and said he would be right back. Pretty soon thereafter I heard a noise like a tractor engine and looked out the window. Sure enough there appeared a John Deere Tractor pulling a red Santa sleigh complete with Christmas lights. I thought we would just have to lift Luke and sit him up front in the seat, but no, Glen had made the sleigh with Luke AND his wheelchair in mind. It had a drop down ramp out the back so Luke could drive right up into it. I still get misty-eyed remembering that Christmas.

All of The Above

I hear many parents say Duchenne wasn't in their plans. My response is that I didn't have a plan. Fourteen years ago I was a going nowhere fast single mom who knew that her life wasn't working but had absolutely no idea how to change it. Then the Duchenne explosion happened and my world changed beyond anything I could have dreamed. Fate led me down a path that has enabled me to live a life that I would not have thought possible.

Glen and I met each other in the good old fashion way: at a bar. He would ask me to dance and I would say no. I had convinced myself that he was not my type because he looked too young and tried too hard. Once, after turning him down, he left and quickly returned with a rose that he had made out of a paper napkin. I had to dance with him then! It was the sweetest gesture that I had ever seen and it sure beat the usual pick up lines. He was a surprisingly great dancer and he liked to talk to me but I still didn't take him seriously for almost two years. I would show up at the bar and he would make a beeline over to me with a paper rose in hand. It was a bit annoying but we would usually spend the evening dancing to every song. Slowly I began to realize that I missed him on those nights that he didn't show up.

My relationship with Glen took a turn on the day that Luke was diagnosed. My cousin Kelley had driven my ex husband Pat and I to the hospital where we heard the news. After we dropped the boys off at Pat's house, Kelley turned to me and asked now what. I said "Take me to the farm," and she said "That's the best damn news I have heard all day."

Up until this point Glen and I had just started dating a bit, but I was taking it very slow and he didn't seem to mind that. He didn't expect anything from me, he seemed to like Luke and the farm where he lived was spectacular. As I mentioned earlier, I was born in the farm's driveway and this made me feel connected to the place. When Kelley and I pulled into the driveway that day, there was Glen in a stark white t-shirt walking up to the house with the sunshine on his back. I ran up to him and he stood there holding me, while I cried my soul out explaining to him what had just happened.

When we drove away I remember thinking that I had most likely just lost him. I suddenly became a lot to take on for a man who was still living at home and had never been married. I thought that being with Luke and I was a guaranteed heartache now, so I was a little taken aback when he called me a week later to see if I needed anything. In my grief, I blurted out that Luke wanted a kitty. Glen brought two. Luke named them Alley Cat and Scaredy Cat.

During those first months post-diagnosis, any time I felt that I was going to die from the pain, Glen would pick me up on his motorcycle and we would ride. On the farm I would walk the fields breathing in the scenery and ride beside him in the tractor. Our relationship began to take on a life of its own. We'd get close and then I would back away. I broke up with Glen several times before I finally figured out that he offered me something that I had never had. Normal. I asked him to bear with me and I am sure glad that he did.

I started calling Glen "All Of The Above" shortly after I realized that I loved him. He fills the broken pieces in my heart. Being with Glen has taught me to love myself.

Chapter Six

Luke and Jenna 2008
This picture says it all. They look so very proud of each other. The love they share is evident.

All About Luke

As Luke's 14th birthday approached, my insides were all bunched up waiting for the other shoe to drop. I started catching myself holding my breath during the day. I was angered easily and was running on nothing but emotion, most of it anger and sadness. Even taking care of Luke's daily needs started to annoy me, which brought on an enormous feeling of guilt. I wanted to be Luke's rock, not an overbearing mother who took her anger and annoyance out on her children. I knew I needed to do something instead of waiting for Luke to die. This wasn't a way to live. And it definitely wasn't fun.

Middle school hell was over for Luke and he was now in high school. Luke enjoyed school more now, but for me, high school brought me a bag full of brand new fears. The high school had more students and thus more commotion, fighting, cliques, etc. How was Luke going to avoid getting hurt physically and emotionally? How could he defend himself? What if he had a medical emergency and no one would help him?

Luke was also going into his freshman year right after his back surgery. We chose the end of the summer, one week before school started, for the surgery so that Luke could enjoy being outside all summer. Even though the timing made things a bit tricky, I felt like I could handle the red tape at school because I was pretty experienced in all things Duchenne by this stage of the game. I had dealt with my son's diagnosis, I had watched him lose his ability to walk, I'd handled a ton of school complications and misunderstandings, not to mention busing issues, in home care issues, and dual household issues.

Before high school started for Luke, I wanted to make sure I hadn't missed anything about going into this new situation and so I called a meeting with Luke's entire new team. Luke needed a male aide to assist him with his school day and he needed an entirely new IEP because his old one was crap! I wanted to take a peek at the new landscape that Luke would be in for the next four years.

Luke's New Hero

Luke and I were crammed into a room with a table much too large for the space. One by one Luke's new team came in and introduced themselves. Then this guy with a twinkle in his eye that I could see even through his glasses smiled at me and said, "Mom, this isn't about you, this is all about Luke, I hope you don't mind." I was relieved and thought "FINALLY someone who gets this whole thing!" The meeting proceeded without any interruption from me. For the first time "Mr School" was talking to Luke and wanting to know what he wanted to get out of high school, his life and his future.

For Luke it was very liberating. After years spent in special education, Luke wanted and needed more. Later, after the meeting, Luke said "I think I am going to like it here. They actually talk to me! I feel like they care."

Later, when Luke met with Mr. School to go over his old Individual Education Plan (IEP). Mr. School read a few things in it and then chucked the entire plan into the garbage can right in front of Luke! He said Luke was smart and didn't need to be in special ed. That day they made a plan to prepare Luke for general education: a plan that would give Luke the tools to advocate for himself. Just in case you don't know, an IEP is a customized educational plan for children with special needs. It gives teachers and school administrators a written guide about the supports such a student needs to receive an equal opportunity education. If it isn't written in the IEP, the school legally doesn't have to do jack for a special needs child. All too often, school districts employ some teachers and staff who don't want to deal with special needs students. The IEP is designed to protect such students and give them the support they need to succeed.

Social Isolation

The social isolation of boys with Duchenne is not intentional but it's a very hard thing to cope with as a parent. I can't put my finger on exactly when it started to happen. It's more like something that slowly creeps into your life that you don't notice until it suddenly slaps you in the face. It's not like other kids aren't nice to Luke, it's just that their activities usually involve physical feats that just aren't possible for him.

When Luke was in middle school, I learned of another boy who lived locally with another type of muscular dystrophy. This boy, Cody, had met Luke at MDA Summer Camp and so Cody's mother and I decided to get the two together. Cody's disease requires a ton of medical equipment and so Luke always went to his house. He stayed all night on a couple of occasions, but then Cody's condition worsened which in turn scared Luke enough to stop going.

As I said, the social isolation is heartbreaking as a parent. Although Luke seems to handle it very well. I know it bothers him to not be included with his peers. We focus on family and Luke has his younger siblings to play with. As a family, we try to keep him busy and include him in as many events we possible. The fact that Luke has two families also helps with the boredom and sort of picks up the slack of not having peers to hang out with.

Luke is constantly surrounded by adults and he is comfortable with that. He has become the master of his own destiny and he gets involved with things of his own choosing, like high school dances. He is learning to say hi and pick up conversations with other students. From talking with other young men living with Duchenne, I gather that college is much better. Luke can't wait.

Down To The Bone

Luke had already been using his wheelchair for a few years full time as his muscles weakened and he lost strength, which is sadly the normal progression of Duchenne. He started favoring one side of his body more and his spine began to curve over causing scoliosis. He was also becoming incontinent and having aches and pain he hadn't had before. Over time if his back went untreated Luke's left lung would most likely collapse. This meant one thing and one thing only. It was time to consider a surgical procedure called spinal fusion where they insert and tie together two titanium rods down both sides of the spine.

Luke's father and I did a lot of research about the surgery and what would likely happen if we opted not to do it. We both felt that there really was no other option. The idea that these were our two options sickened me further and backed me into a corner ripping my heart and mind right in two. I had always felt that I would instinctively know when it was Luke's time to pass, but when I had to decide whether to go ahead with Luke's full spinal fusion surgery, my insecurities bombarded me and I wavered. So many questions loomed before me and I wondered if I had done everything possible for my boy. "Would I lose my baby during surgery? Did we wait too long? What is life going to be like after the surgery? Will he still be able to feed himself?" Any surgery is very risky for a DMD boy because of complications that can arise from the use of anesthesia.

These questions kept plaguing me and I often woke up sweaty and scared out of my mind. As I mentioned earlier, I had a premonition years before that Luke would not live past the age of 14 and at the time of the surgery, he was not quite 15!

Another thing making me crazy about the surgery was the timing of it. At the end of the summer, harvest in Alaska is in full swing and that meant that I would be facing Luke's surgery without Glen, my number one support person. I was absolutely terrified!

Once Luke went into surgery, the agony of waiting was excruciating and I was an emotional wreck. I sat waiting with my mom, my sister and my aunt. Luke's dad, Pat, and his new girlfriend Bessie sat in a windowed nook some distance away. Every so often Pat would walk past me to the bathroom with a sick look on his face. The stress heightened when I looked up to find several of my family members all walk in at the same time looking like they had lost their best friend. My heart dropped. "Did they know something I didn't?"

I found out soon enough that my family had just received news that a cousin had gone over a ravine in his car and was found two days later, alive but in need of surgery. Ironically, he had been helicoptered to the same hospital and was waiting on Luke's operating room!

In all, Luke's surgery was 9 hours long. He spent a total of 8 days in the hospital and he only needed 8 weeks of bed rest at home before returning back to school instead of the standard 12 weeks normally required for recovery from such surgery. He healed very quickly. In recovery I unexpectedly witnessed love in its truest form. The doctor had just removed the breathing tube from Luke's lungs and Luke was sort of freaking out. My ex husband's girlfriend Bessie started rubbing Luke's hand with tears streaming down her face. My heart overflowed with amazement and joy at seeing another women, another mom, love my boy entirely! I was and still am delighted that Pat found a keeper.

During Luke's recovery at home I was opening a can when the sharp metal circle came up and cut my finger. I actually heard it nick the bone! I was jumping around the kitchen holding my finger and screaming. "I cut my finger, I cut my finger all the way down to the bone!" Luke said, "That is nothing, I'll show you down to the bone!" So true! Luke's scar starts at his neck and runs all the way down to his tail bone where the rods were placed on both sides of his spine and screwed into his hip bones. When I first saw the stitches I thought I was going to pass out! Another piece of my heart broken. How was that possible? I didn't think I had anything left in there to break!

With Luke resting peacefully, I went to take a shower in the "family" shower at the hospital when I completely broke down, in shock from the horror of what my boy had just endured! What I had allowed to happen to him! But without the surgery, Luke would have been bedridden from pain and he would have had great difficulty breathing. If we had not straightened it, his spine would have slowly crushed his organs and lungs. It's a decision that no mother should ever have to make!

Run For Our Sons

When I first heard of this fundraising event by Parent Project Muscular Dystrophy, the title alone enticed me to enter the January 2006 Disney World Marathon in Orlando, Florida. What an empowering feeling to join in a cause to help someone else, especially your very own child. And even more so when you see others joining in for your cause.

However, running a marathon meant training and training in Alaska meant winter training, which I had never done, let alone ever running an entire marathon. But I threw caution to the wind and decided to commit to run a half marathon, 13.1 miles. I got right to work and set up my First Giving fundraising page and friends started jumping in with donations. As far as training, every morning off I'd go. I hated it, but I persevered by thinking that I was doing something for Luke that he could not do himself. It also was better than sitting around watching Luke's body deteriorate.

It was very neat to be a part of something bigger. For the first time I didn't feel so alone. I felt someone finally understood. On the night before marathon day the temperature dropped down in the low 30's. I wasn't prepared for cold at all. You'd think coming from Alaska I would have known better, but I was in the land of Florida orange juice and I was expecting warm sunshine! I have never been so cold in my life!

Nothing prepared me for the feeling of amazement that I got when I stepped off the bus at the start line. I could feel the energy in the air. I arrived early because I had no idea what to expect. There I was, this country bumpkin of a girl born and raised in a small Alaskan town and suddenly I was literally engulfed by thousands of people! UNBELIEVABLE!

And then we were off. What a feeling! I ran the first part of my race with tears streaming down my face. As daylight hit, I came around a turn and looked back at the runners all around me. I was awestruck. Suddenly I felt very small and life seemed so big, so real. Would our efforts be enough to find a cure in my son's life time? Or what about my future grandchildren?

All of these thoughts came and went, then up ahead was Cinderella's castle. But instead of feeling like a princess I felt sharp stomach pains and they didn't feel like the normal cramps that you get from running. When I finally got to a bathroom stop, I discovered the culprit: My monthly friend came in the middle of the marathon! I wasn't prepared for that. I didn't have any money on me to purchase what I needed. I was, as the saying goes, up a creek without a paddle! There I sat on the toilet crying...I had to finish, I was so close. What was I going to do? I folded toilet paper and decided to walk the rest of the way.

At 11 miles my legs were on fire, screaming at me in pain. At 12 miles I was ready to throw in the towel as I kept worrying that I was making a mess that other people could notice. Down to the last .1 of a mile, which at the time felt like another 10! I could no longer feel my legs at all. Just then I heard the crowd roar and I knew the finish line was close. I started my hobbling attempt to run across the finish line with arms outstretched. I did it! I felt accomplishment and bewilderment at the same time. I received my Donald Duck Medal and it is proudly displayed on Luke's wall next to his Dale Ernhart Jr. poster.

Possibilities

On the Duchenne front I was meeting grown men living well into their 20s and even 30s. For the first time I realized that I was living in the box that the DMD diagnosis tries to put over your life. The "truths" that I had always believed about Luke's future were falling apart. Ideas like: There is no cure, Luke won't live past age 14, he will never have children or a mate to love him. Those parameters are so limiting! Life can be so strange and full of mystery.

As I was *awakening* and looking back over the last several years it seemed like every time I hit a block or a hard point, life opened up with what I needed right at the very moment that I needed it. I slowly was beginning to realize that Luke was going to live much longer than 14 years. It was apparent that I needed to prepare myself and Luke for a future, hopefully a long one. I submitted my application to The Partners in Policy Making (PIP) Internship program. For the last 20 years PIP has been teaching parents and self advocates the power of advocacy to change the world's perception of people living with disabilities. To change the way they are supported, viewed and taught. Taking the course was a major mental shift for me. Instead of waiting for Luke to die, I was suddenly preparing for his future. The course was so good for me. Not only did it teach me about the vast opportunities for Luke, it also opened my eyes to ways that I could fulfill my yearning to help other people.

Buggy Time

The winter before Mothers Day of 06 Glen was locked away after work in his shop working tirelessly on a project that would get Luke from the yard to the mountains and surrounding mud holes. The best of Alaska is seen off the beaten trail and just because Luke was in a wheelchair wasn't going to stop Glen from figuring out another way for us all to build memories. With Luke, the favorite memories usually involve wheels, mud and family.

That was how "Luke's Buggy" was born. Using an old garbage truck that had been given to us, Glen built a flat deck with a driver's seat, back seat for the girls and wheelchair lift that he found in someone's junk pile.

Luke has gone where few have ever traveled before because of the buggy. My dream of the Alaska outdoor lifestyle for Luke is a reality and I have Glen to thank. During the summer if we aren't farming or hanging out on the deck, we are on Luke's buggy. We pack up the cooler, throw in the rubber tote that I fill with coats, blankets, toilet paper, bug spray, survival food and anything else I can think of 'just in case' and head for the river or up to the Jones's Ville Coal Mine Road to go find some scenery and hopefully some MUD!

The buggy has been featured in the National MDA Quest magazine in an article titled "Born To Be Wild." It's also on the MDA website.

Another Surgery

The muscle loss in Luke's body combined with the fact that he sits in his wheelchair pretty much all day made Luke's body start to curl inward. The back surgery fixed his back but his feet were turning inward and upward too. Shoes began to really bother him and he didn't like the way his feet began to look. So we decided to go in for heel cord lengthening surgery, figuring it would be a piece of cake compared to his nine hour back surgery.

The surgery was only about an hour from start to finish, but the aftermath was horrendous. Luke was in such severe pain after the surgery and the pain medication didn't seem to help at all. He laid there crying while everyone around him tried to make him comfortable. It was horrible for me to watch and hear my child laying there in pain that I could do nothing to change. I felt so powerless and the mother bear in me came out with a vengeance. Those poor nurses.

Steven

Luke first met Steven at school, then again at MDA Summer Camp, and from time to time we would run into him and his family at the MDA Clinic and other MDA functions like the Jerry Lewis Labor Day Telethon.

We had just seen Steven at clinic a couple of weeks before when the call came in that Steven had died. I was driving down the road and it was pouring down rain. I closed my cell phone and pulled over and sobbed for Steven's mother and the loss that she must feel. I cried for the relief I felt that it wasn't Luke. I cried for Steven. I screamed out "NO MORE BOYS!"

A few days later at the funeral I watched Steve's brother and family carry in his casket. It was dark gray with Steve's baseball hats on top. I couldn't help but think that could be Luke. I reached for Luke's hand for a squeeze to reassure myself Luke was okay. During the service, the minister said it saddened him to think that the spot where Steven parked his wheelchair every Sunday would be empty, that today would have been the first time. The minister went on to day that when he entered the church, low and behold, another young man has honored his spot. There were two spots for wheelchairs to park next to the pews in the Church. Luke just so happened to pick the place where Steven had parked his. I lost it then, tears streamed down my face along with my mascara. Steve's death hit too close to home.

Later, as we were driving away, Luke told me he sort of wished he hadn't gone. He said it was a lot harder than he had imagined. I told him I was sorry and that I really hadn't known what to expect since we weren't that close and hardly knew Steven and his family.

Sweet 16

As Luke approached his 16th birthday, I felt so thankful that he was still with us and that he was happy and enjoying his life. I got together with Bessie and we planned a Nascar Mexican Surprise Birthday Party for Luke. We rented a local community hall big enough to hold both of his entire families and we brought in all of his favorite people, foods, and activities. For me, the best part of the whole experience was being able to plan it with such an awesome stepmom. Bessie makes sure that Luke is being taken care of like he is her own son. I love having her around and our situation works very well for Luke, which we both agree is the most important thing in the world.

To Give up or FIGHT, that is the question

When it comes to medical treatments and interventions related to the progression of Duchenne, Luke always resists and can be very stubborn. Sometimes it is like pulling teeth to get Luke to agree about what should be done. I have always felt that Luke should make his own decisions when it comes to his body. I try to lay out the facts and show him my research results, tell him my opinion and go from there. When Dr. Lungs suggested it was time for night time breathing assistance, Luke immediately put up a wall. I was so frustrated because I knew he needed help and that it would improve how he was feeling, but I could not get him to make a decision. I ordered the bi-pap anyway and started to think about how I could make it seem like a good option to Luke.

The situation suddenly became much more urgent when a few days later, I picked Luke up from school after he had spent several days at his dad's house. I saw him and was struck by how horrible he looked! As his mom, I knew something was up. We were on our way to an ear appointment and since we were already at the hospital, I decided to take him to the emergency room to see what was going on. Luke had a fit and fought me the entire time, telling me that he was fine, just a little sick.

It turned out that "a little sick" was full blown pneumonia with fever, cough, and the works. I was worried sick but still had to drop Luke back off at his dad's because it wasn't my week to have him. Once he arrived back at my house a few days later, I told him that he had to try the bi-pap for one hour a night. I told him that I would stay with him until he could tolerate it. He told me that he wasn't going to do it and I responded by saying that I would sleep on the floor of his room if I had to. He still refused to do it and I went to my room exasperated. A few minutes later I stormed back into Luke's room and had "the talk."

I know this usually means telling your teenager about sex but with a Duchenne teenager, it sometimes means "the talk" of life and death. I said, "Remember you told me you were going to fight? Well, what's it gonna be? Are you going to fight or give up?" There was a long pause before he yelled, "I'm gonna fight damn it"! Then we just cried together. He decided that the bipap wasn't so bad after all. He actually loves it now. When he first puts in on at night, his eyes roll back, he takes several large breaths and says, "Ahhh, this feels so good."

Jenna Benna

During my 9 months of pregnancy with Jenna, I spent lots of time thinking about what I wanted for her. I tried very hard not to have dreams about sugar and spice and everything little girls are made of. I knew from my experience with Luke that sometimes life has different ideas.

But one of the things I did know was that I didn't expect Jenna to take care of Luke. I wanted her to have her own identity, free of any obligations other than the normal responsibilities that go with being a member of a family. Of course Glen and I realized that Jenna would have challenges in her life because of the situation with Luke. That's why we have always tried to provide her with a strong support network of family and good friends. She is very close to her grandparents, including adopted grandmother Elinor, her aunts and uncles and her cousins.

As a baby, she was an exuberant bundle of joy and determination and she has transformed into a young girl who is sensitive, fun, smart, witty and compassionate. I never sugar coated Luke's diagnosis but looking back, I see that it might have been wise to shelter her a bit from the truth when she was very young. When she was in first and second grade, she Jenna began to realize that Luke might die. She started sleeping in Luke's bed when he was away at his dad's house and her grades suffered terribly. She also whined a lot and I believe the emotions running through her were just too much to bear.

During one heart to heart conversation, Jenna told me that she was scared that Luke would die without her, that he would leave without saying goodbye, that she wouldn't know. I held her close and told her she would be one of the very first to hear when it was Luke's time to pass. My heart was squeezed so tight in my chest from keeping back the tears because Jenna needed me to be strong for her. She needed to feel comfort.

We held her back in second grade in order to give her more time to mature emotionally and I stopped taking her to Luke's doctor appointments. Glen and I also started spending more time with just her. Glen takes her to school in the morning for quality dad time and Jenna and I paint our toes, go hiking or go shopping together all the time. As a family we watch movies and play games together and in the summertime, we are always outside on our buggy or walking the vegetable fields.

Jenna's love for her brother is evident and she does help out with Luke, but it's by choice and not obligation. As Duchenne has taken over Luke's body, their play has changed and adapted. She does the physical stuff like putting the legos together while Luke supervises and comes up with new and innovative ideas. They spend hours talking and she loves to watch Luke play his video games.

As for me, I love having a daughter who is all giggles and pinkness, who cares deeply about matching outfits and shoes. Our talks about our hopes and dreams are different and I am so thankful that she can turn to me when she needs me. It is also an incredible experience to not worry about her health, although the fact that she might be a carrier of Duchenne is of concern to me. One day, she can find out her status and decide on her own future with regard to children. I did not have a choice and I want it to be different for my daughter. What can I say, she is my girl.

You Might Be a Red Neck If

Luke loves anything with Jeff Foxworthy, Larry the Cable Guy and the Here's Your Sign guy, Bill Engvall. Luke even went through a time writing his own red neck stories. He loves pretty much anything redneck, including NASCAR.

No matter where he is, every weekend of Nascar Season, from February through November, he sits in front of the TV watching "the channel" that is broadcasting the latest race. Luke screams at the TV and tells the announcers to shut up and get on with the race.

Luke is a Forever Junior Nation fan all the way! He can spout off driver statistics, car details and who is leading in whatever car series. This is way over my head, but I have such fun watching Luke doing things that he loves to do. The only thing that comes before Nascar in the summer is the weather outside.

For Christmas last year Pat and Bessie bought Luke tickets to see a live Nascar race in Las Vegas, Nevada! Once again, I just cried at this news. It will definitely be a dream come true for Luke, another thing checked off his "bucket list."

Luke's Bump

When you live all your life in a small town, you get to know the area. You know where things are without even knowing the names of the roads. Every winter heading down the off ramp to Palmer, there is a gigantic frost heave that gets bigger and bigger over time. Luke dreads this ginormous bump, which has become enemy number one since his back surgery. He has injured his back several times and worries about it daily. He will remind you EVERY time about the bump. Riding the school bus is even worse. Luke is also very intuitive about people and he can tell if someone is sincere or mean hearted or not understanding. I have gotten in the habit of asking Luke what he thinks about certain people because he is always right.

When he started his junior year he had a new bus driver who he did not care for from the beginning. He said he was grumpy and drove too fast. Strike one! Heading down the off ramp home after school one afternoon, Luke's bump loomed up ahead and Luke told the bus driver to slow down. Luke said the guy looked right at him and didn't slow down at all. They hit the bump so hard that Luke's wheelchair, all 500+ pounds of it, came up off the floor. Luke came smashing down into his seat and jarred his back. It took several weeks to heal. Strike 2!

The mother bear in me reared her head again and I came unglued. I reported the incident immediately and the bus driver had to attend safety classes all during Christmas break. They even made him sit in a wheelchair blindfolded and drove him around. Ahh, sweet justice!.

Jello Shooters

Social Isolation is one of the challenges Luke has had to face and as a parent, I try to figure out ways for Luke to be included with his peers. Sports, driving and high school parties don't happen for Luke. He is the only student in his entire school who has just a physical disability without other mental or cognitive issues. He is mainstreamed with regular education classes and he has friends, but Luke is never included or invited over to anyone's home and he's left out of trips to the movies or the mall. Most high school students don't have the forethought or resources to include Luke.

Our friends the Cottinni's completely understand the social isolation issue. Last year on our annual trip to their cabin, someone had the bright idea to make Jello Shooters with peach jello and a little peach schnapps. Luke had one but Glen and his friend Pio did this hilarious act that had Luke believing that they were really drunk. Luke is no dummy, and he immediately realized that he depended on these two men to get him around at the cabin. The two of them actually attach Luke's sling to a metal pole and carry him back and forth between the main house and the guest cabin, where we stay. Pio especially was stumbling around, laughing and joking with everyone. They teased Luke right up until bedtime. Luke was too nice to say anything but his face said it all.

Even after Pio told Luke he was just joking around Luke was still very skeptical. We all tried to help Luke feel more comfortable but the more we did the more Luke didn't believe us. We were all laughing. Luke laughs about it now and feels incredible that he has friends who try so hard to give him fun experiences.

It wasn't long enough

Luke's first Prom was symbolic in that I didn't think I would get to experience seeing him attend. Not only was he attending Prom, his date was drop dead gorgeous. I was helping him dress which was no easy feat with Luke's contractions in his elbows. I could hardly get his arm through the tux jacket sleeve. I helped him with his hair with tears in my eyes, while his dad washed up the van. Luke looked so handsome in his tux.

Before Prom, we had decided to take everyone out for dinner at Luke's favorite restaurant, so Bessie, Luke, his date, my daughter and I all piled into the van and headed out. In keeping with the high spirit of the evening, some of us adults ordered drinks while we looked at the menu. The waitress, who seemed very nervous about Luke's wheelchair, came with the drinks and then the unthinkable happened.

She dropped my entire drink all over Luke and his wheelchair. I jumped to action and flew open his tux jacket to hopefully flip off the drink, but his right arm (his driving arm) and joy stick were soaked! I closed my eyes and took a breath so I could get control of my emotions.

I had to take off his jacket which I barely had gotten on him in the first place and I wasn't sure if I could get it off with it being wet. I washed his shirt sleeve while it was still on his body but then his arm started getting a rash from the drink and the wheelchair wouldn't turn on. Prom was totally not going to happen without his wheelchair. The waitress kept apologizing saying she would go get the manager. Not only was dinner on the house but they also offered to pay the cleaning bill for the tux. Luke's date was so mad that she ordered the most expensive thing on the menu and shared it with my daughter.

Dinner didn't taste as good as it normally did and frankly, we all thought the night was a bust. I said "Lets eat and let the joystick dry" while Luke kept telling us that his chair had better turn on. I kept thinking, "oh please start" but I had no idea what to do if it didn't. I knew we would get home but I wasn't sure if I could help Luke through this disappointment. I joked, saying they wouldn't let Luke into prom smelling like alcohol. I got a smile out of him but that was it.

To all of our surprise, Luke's chair started! It acted a little strange and Luke said, "I think my wheelchair is a little drunk!" At least his sense of humor and optimism were back! The wheelchair wasn't working perfectly but it seemed good enough to go and his shirt sleeve was almost dry.

I am sure my eyes glistened with moisture as we dropped Luke and his date off at Prom. Jenna loved watching the rainbow of pretty dresses. Luke wheeled himself down the corridor and I just smiled, feeling incredible for him. He is the one who wanted to go to Prom with or without a date and here he was doing a "normal" teenage thing! I couldn't have been more proud.

When driving home I could hear the marvel in Luke's voice talking about Prom. He said it went by too quick, even though it was 2 am by the time we arrived at home. I took his jacket off one more time and I asked him if he had been drinking. He laughed and said "I don't drink and drive."

Chapter Seven

Luke and Ken Summer 2009
How wonderful to see, other than the wheelchair Luke looks so
healthy. Picture taken after Ken the cat decides he would jump up
on Luke's lap. It happen so fast Luke was laughing from being
startled.

Life Goes On

L uke is a bight individual who is almost always focused on the positive except when he thinks he has been wronged. He is stubborn when it comes to his care, especially his medical care. He has to be pushed into a corner before he decides anything. Truth be known I would be the same way. Now that he is older, he thinks things through and is ready to give his opinion when asked. When he gets bored, frustrated or is on a mission he gets lippy and pushes his limits like any normal teenager. Then the next moment he is completely sharing his love. Every day he tells me he loves me. He can be annoying, argumentative and has a way to drive me straight up the wall! He is insightful and sees beauty all around him and is ready to share it, like the shape of a leaf or the pattern on a waiting room chair that reminds him of a crowd of people.

Sometimes when I am dressing him the impact of Duchenne on his body sickens me, saddens me, frustrates me and ultimately makes me angry. The feeling is so powerful that I catch myself being rough, impatient and angry. It's like this invisible force takes over and I react and immediately feel guilt and remorse wash through me. I want to be Luke's "rock." During his early teen years this was almost a daily experience. Now I often go months without an outburst and then his leg will flop a certain way, or his fingers will get stuck, or his sling is difficult to put on, or I spill the pee and snap! I realize now what I feel is normal and when I feel overwhelmed there is usually a very valid reason. I talk with Luke and we figure out the solution together. More times than not it is because I am tired. Initially it was because I needed more help with Luke's care. I am getting better in how I handle myself and I am able to tell Luke how I am feeling, not to make him feel bad but for him to understand. Luke has a saying "Communication is Rocket Science" and we try hard to keep the communication open. Sometimes we fail, sometimes we get it right. Isn't that what families do?

As Luke's "care manager" I know Luke's needs, wants and desires. I know his rights and more importantly I am his mom and I have every right to make sure that he is taken care of. On the flip side however, I have also made sure that Luke knows how to take care of himself. I have prepared him to think about himself and expect other people to do things for him. He needs others to take care of his physical needs but that does not mean that they have a say so over him.

Duchenne sucks but life still goes on, love needs to be shared, bills need to be paid and 365 dinners need to be made a year.

Yard work

Our summer season in Alaska is only about 12 weeks long. Even into April we still have snow. The minute grass starts poking through here and there Alaskans start spring yard work and the outdoor get togethers begin. By June and July summer is in full swing and we all pray for the snow to melt off the mountains before the end of August. Sometimes it happens, sometimes we get lucky. One year, my husband cut down some small trees and underbrush in the front of our house to open up the view of Pioneer Peak. Luke and Jenna had this idea that they could use a rope tied to the brush and trees and Luke could pull them over to the burn pile using his wheelchair. I did some but Luke, his aide and Jenna worked on the pile for 3 or 4 days. Luke was so proud to be able to do something to help out around the house.

Hell And Back

It was the last week of August 2009 and the sun was shining, no wind whipped the tips of the leaves that were just starting to turn yellow and that meant a perfect day for a buggy trip. We headed up to the Jonesville Coal Mine Road to check out part of the trail we hadn't seen in some time. It was a glorious day and we stopped and ate lunch, viewed wild mountain goats through the scope, and explored old drill holes made by the coal miners back in the day when they used to dynamite the mountain.

As usual, we waved at all the other locals enjoying what would most likely be the last summer day we would have for 7 long months. As we were leaving, Glen noticed a trail leading off through a man made canyon wall and decided we should go check it out. On the side of one wall someone had sprayed painted the words "Wecome to Hell" in graffiti-like letters. We just laughed and thought yeah right, scary!

Once in the canyon we saw these two guys, one driving through this large mud hole on a four wheeler covered from head to toe in mud and the other filming his buddy tearing up the mud hole, sending clumps of mud and water flying. We watched them and thought we would have no problem having some fun in that mud ourselves.

Glen drove into the mud hole slowly and everything seemed fine. Wrong! Suddenly we felt the buggy sink right up to the frame, tires turning like large useless chocolate donuts. Normally I would be doing the freaked out mom thing but all I could do was laugh and grab my mud boots. We had to figure out how in the heck we were going to get out of this mess!

We always take a winch with us but as we looked around, we noticed that there were absolutely no trees anywhere close enough for us to use. Thankfully about 100 yards away there were some large boulders. We slowly winched the buggy out with big slurpy mud sounds the entire way. Luke is a chip off the old block and was so calm in his faith that Glen would get us out of there. We took a picture of the graffiti on our way out. Whoever wrote those words weren't kidding! Welcome to hell alright!

Don't die without me

Two weeks after the homecoming dance Luke and 400 other students ended up with the flu. Young men with DMD are respiratorily impaired, so this illness landed Luke in the hospital for 9 days. Prior to what we fondly refer to as "Luke's vacation" was a week of 3 emergency room visits, major sleep deprivation, high stress and me being scared out of my mind. Luke had a fever, he wouldn't eat, his heart rate was through the roof and he was more stubborn about going to the doctor than I had ever seen him before.

Outwardly, Jenna seemed to be doing fine. She prayed for Luke every night but she seemed well otherwise. I finally put my foot down after several days of Luke's stubbornness and told Luke that he had no choice: We were heading into Anchorage to the Providence Hospital. His in-home care support person loaded the van and I went to the bathroom when the phone rang. Luke can't pick up the phone on his own so the recorder came on. It was Jenna, crying and saying "Mom I really need to talk to you, pick up the phone, I am scared, I don't want Luke to die without me." With my heart crumbling into a million pieces yet again, I came out of the bathroom to find Luke moved emotionally. He had tears in his eyes and said "I didn't realize how worried she was."

Hospital Blessing

Luke was emitted to the hospital immediately. He was dehydrated and his potassium level was dangerously low. Low potassium causes lack of appetite and lactic acid build up in the muscles, causing the body to hurt all over. He also had the flu and pneumonia. They told us that he would most likely have long term respiratory damage, which meant we should be thinking about a tracheotomy. This was never an option that we even wanted to consider. I so wanted Luke to finish high school without any major medical issues. I was super emotional and in mother bear mode. I held it together for Luke but once I left the room to talk on the phone or take a walk I would breakdown. I was scared for Luke, for Jenna and the rest of the family.

After 3 days spent at the hospital, I was exhausted and just wanted to sleep on the makeshift pull out bed that I had made beside Luke's bed. The doctor had told him that if he used his cough assist machine with the respiratory team every hour on the hour to cough out the fluid in his lungs he could go home. This was all Luke needed to hear. He put his entire being into following the doctor's orders. He coughed every hour on the hour for a day and a half until he couldn't cough anymore. Watching him put his mind to something and fight is a memory imprinted in my mind for life. I swell with pride thinking about how hard he worked and at the same time it made me indescribably sad. I could not do this for him. I could not take his pain away this time. I had to force myself to remember that if you help a butterfly out of its cocoon it will die.

As I laid there praying for sleep to take me for a few hours, Luke just would not stop talking. Looking back on it, I am pretty sure he thought that if he kept talking nothing bad was going to happen to him. I kept thinking "Please Luke, shut up! I need some rest." After a few minutes of silence, he said "Mom are you asleep yet? I said "No" and what he said next melted my heart. He said, "I love you Mom, I don't know what I would do without you." I am so glad that I stayed awake long enough to hear such heavenly words. I cried and said "I know".

My sister had been driving an hour almost every day to visit either before work or after. One day before she left she asked if we could all pray together. The blessing she gave was from the heart and touched both Luke and I deeply. Luke said he felt very much loved and that everything was going to be okay. He also said that, in a way, our hospital vacation had been kind of fun. I said, minus the stress it was fun, just him and I hanging out, watching movies but more importantly having time with just the two of us. Our human to human, friend to friend, mother to child bond became stronger than ever. I wouldn't call myself a religious person but I am deeply spiritual. I believe we are all connected. Everything happens for a reason even though events don't always make sense at the moment they occur. Life is an amazing journey full of transformation and awakening. But the religious blessing from my sister that day brought me such comfort and peace that I want to share it. I am truly grateful for it.

*Father God, I first want to start off by thanking
You for blessing us with Luke. Lord,
You knew what You were doing when You sent
him into our lives! I have learned
From Luke to treat each day as it's your last and
to live it up! He is SO strong and I know
that only comes from You. Father as Luke and
Misty
face this next step in life,
Lord I ask for Your direction. I ask that
You would be with the doctors, give them
the knowledge and wisdom to know what to do
next.
Lord bless them for all that they do. Father
I ask that
You would direct both Luke and
Misty and help them make the right medical
choice for Luke.
Father you are an amazing
God and the great physician. I ask that Your will,
will be done in this situation and rest to come
when it
comes to Luke's life.
Father give Luke the rest he needs to heal and
help him to stay strong. Lord I again praise
Your name for Luke and the blessing I have to be
his aunt.*

Lord. You are in control and I ask that You would give
Misty and Luke the peace of knowing that.
I say these things in Your glorious and
precious name. Amen

My Doggie

We'd barely been home a week from "Luke's Vacation" when Glen came in from feeding our dog Max and said that he wasn't eating. I called our vet, who is a family friend, and she came over for a home visit the next day. We ended up taking him to her clinic for x rays and we discovered that his bladder was as big as a watermelon, pushing his intestines up toward his heart. The outlook was not good for our beloved pet of 13 years and we decided to put him down. I took him home to spend some time with Luke and Jenna before the vet come to euthanize him.

The yellow and orange leaves of fall were all over the ground next to his dog house where he spent his final minutes in my arms. Jenna sat on top of the dog house and Luke sat nearby as Max took his last breaths. I was crying, Jenna was crying, then Luke started crying. This was all it took for the vet to start crying. We were all blubbering like big babies. Max was part of the family. Luke, trying to be the tough man, finally broke down and sobbed, "My doggie!"

Class Ring

"Can you believe your boy is a Senior Mom?" Luke asked me coming into the house after school recently. I simply answered "No," but in my mind I wondered if he knew the significance of his words. He then said, "Guess what? I brought home all of the order forms for my cap and gown, but you can order the ring online. It's so cool! You can even design it on a website!" Luke bugged me all night, so finally I caved in. He was right, it was very cool and it only took about 30 minutes for us to design the ring he wanted.

I told Luke I wasn't going to wear any makeup for graduation because all I'm going to do is cry the entire time. I never thought I would be see him graduate. I had prepared myself during all of these years that he might be gone by the time most kids graduate and here we were, just four months away from the big day. Luke says he is sad to leave behind his teachers, aides and therapists. He also says he feels like he just started high school because it's only been two years since he was mainstreamed.

Advocating

Since recently taking charge of his life, Luke says he has woken up to the *real world*. I couldn't be more proud of him. I consider Luke living to 18 and experiencing graduation with him to be one of the life's highest honors. What a wonderful sight to witness Luke training his own aides and support people, taking care of his own scheduling and remembering everything he needs to transport himself from one household to the other. He keeps us all on our toes and is always thinking ahead and looking on the bright side. Luke is Mr. Positive ninety percent of the time and he has a great outlook on life. He loves his life, his family and has dreams for the future. He plans to take Autocad since he loves to design and create things. Alaska is a young state and it is one of the few that is growing, so Autocad will come in handy when he starts looking for a job. He actually already has a job with an engineering firm and he hasn't even taken a lick of college. And Oh, did I mention, Luke is a poet.

This Place

When Luke was first diagnosed I used to go to a place where I'd walk through fields of vegetables and nap in grassy meadows with the power and energy of majestic mountains standing like protective giants of my mind, body and spirit. A place where I could rejuvenate my heart and soul. I needed to be with what I knew was real, what I could see, what I could touch and smell. The earth, the sunshine, the gentle breeze on my face. It is the place I was born and now the place I live, laugh and love. The place where Glen grew up and then to which he introduced me and offered to share. A place Luke instantly fell in love with as a little boy. VanderWeele Farms spoke to my heart the very first time I set foot on her fields, took in the beauty of her scenery and the glory of Pioneer Peak.

Luke wrote this poem for his poetry class which showcases perfectly what the farm means to him. He calls it "This Place".

There is a place on the farm
To get away from it all
This place has a certain charm
Open and free with no walls
Green rows that go on for miles
Topped with white flowers so high
A landscape so beautiful and wild
Yet not like the days gone by
Surrounding the field of green and white
A dirt road weaves and whines
Standing tall the fireweed is such a sight
A more perfect place is hard to find
The irrigation sprinklers spray the mist
The heat of the day shines down from above
The water beads on leaves it's kissed
And moistens the ground that was tilled with love
Such a sunny day with puffy white clouds
A slight breeze sings through the leaves

Of trees that stand so tall and proud
And still so much more to see
With Pioneer Peak rising to the sky
What an incredible and glorious day
An eagle soars on wings so high
This place just takes your breath away!

Let There Be Light

January brings bitter cold clear blue nights. Often the fog will settle over the land as it did just a few short months ago, frosting the trees and anything else in its path. On one such night recently, I was sitting by the Christmas tree looking out at it all. The moon was out, sending its glow over the ice crystals that had gathered on the deck. They sparkled like a field of diamonds. As if reading my mind Luke said from behind me, "Aren't they beautiful Mom?" I of course replied "yes they are son." The meaning of Luke is: He who brings light. What a fitting name for my son, for it is absolutely true.

Chapter Eight

VanderWeele Farms
**This Place Every time I see this picture I want to take a walk. This
is the view I see every day.**

A Dedication To All Duchenne Parents

I have spent years trying to understand the "why's" and put realistic perspective on Luke being diagnosed with a incurable life threatening disease. I didn't and still don't want to believe there is nothing I can do about it. Maybe medicine can't yet, but I certainly have to the power if I choose to getup each and every day to be the best I can be, despite the pain.

So I started digging into the subjects of natural healing, healing of the heart and death, in particular what really happens to us when we die. I have read several books about the soul's path, different books about mediums and numerous books on nutrition, the law of attraction, the power of the subconscious mind and energy of the body. I have taken a phone conference course titled "Discover the Heart" which I highly recommend by Diane Vela creator of "Programs of the Heart." I then went on to dabble into what's called energy work of the body. I can't go into detail exactly the type of energy work I was doing with myself and both my children. The ground breaking work is still highly controversial and I signed an agreement not to give exacts and particulars. But the energy work of the body is incredible. Dr Oz has recently quoted *"We're beginning to understand things that we know in our heart are true but we could never measure, "he says."As we get better at understanding how little we know about the body,we begin to realize that the next big frontier, in medicine is energy medicine. It's not the mechanistic parts moving. It's not the chemistry of our body. It's understanding for the first time how energy influences how we feel."*

Simply put the energy work we were doing is you ask your body certain questions and you learn how to read your bodies answers by listening, trusting and "feeling" what is truth. The questions are very probing and thought provoking, like did Luke and I chose this the life path of Duchenne together or can we change the direction of our path once chosen. I know this sounds crazy but often times Luke and I are looking so deep into each others eyes I am not sure if I am feeling his soul or if it is mine, the connection is so vast. As you can imagine this brings up fear, pain, and tears. These probing questions and the actual process of the work has deepened my relationship with Luke, not many parents get to probe the depths of our child's soul let alone get to ask deep life questions. I am forever grateful to have this opportunity. A resource about the healing energy of the body, that I find useful and that I highly recommend is called "The Healing Codes" which can be found at http://MistyVanderWeele.com.

Luke loves the work, he always breaths better and his body functions at a higher energy after each session. He tells me it just "feels good" We probably should be doing the work everyday instead of falling back on it with questions in times of crisis, but try to do the work at least once a week.

The energy work brings out the spirit of the soul for exploration in a safe manner, we can talk about the heavy stuff like death freely and the small stuff openly, knowing what we ask is all in the name of love and healing. It is very beautiful.

I hope one day very soon this work will be available for everyone who is willing and open minded. There is so much we don't know about how our bodies work about the spark that keeps us on living. Life is such a mystery.

I wish with my entire being that I could offer you a way out of the relentless agony that Duchenne bestows on your life. I alone don't have that power. The only thing that will end Duchenne and its impact on your life is it's end.

As you navigate through the depths of Duchenne's progression, know that you aren't alone. I am willing to bet that every emotion you are feeling is completely normal. Please know that the ever present pain you feel won't kill you. It just feels like it sometimes.

Living through the different stages of Duchenne is much like grief. You receive the diagnosis and, although there is shock and disbelief, your child is still very young and the effects are only slightly present, so you cruise along like everything is sort of fine.

Next you go to a clinic and you get AFO's and maybe start steroids. You deal with these new conditions and you keep on living and paying the bills. Before you know it, it is time for the first wheelchair and you think life will never be the same. You are right but surprised that this chair on wheels that you had always thought was tragic actually makes life easier for a while. Well at least until you decide to go anywhere.

Then you go on living until the clinic visit when you learn that your child's lung capacity is starting to decline. You go home sad, a little angry and a lot scared. But things keep on keeping on until you notice that your child's posture may be learning to one side and sure enough, it's time for spinal fusion back surgery. WHAT?, you think, "Things were going so well." The dreaded surgery and recovery come and go. Finally a breather, or so you thought.

Other surgeries may be necessary, as was the case with Luke's heel cord lengthening procedure. So many things can go wrong, like problems with anesthesia and intolerable pain that you can't do a damn thing about. So you settle in and try to focus on keeping your child healthy and all will be well. Then pneumonia strikes for the first time and you get lucky because your kid is able to escape hospitalization and kick it on his own. YEAH! That is until your child gets it again and this time lands in the hospital where he may or may not get a tracheotomy. Somehow you find your way again, hoping there will be a cure in your child's lifetime.

It is normal to feel anger, rage, guilt, compassion, sadness, deep soul wrenching pain and grief. But through this pain you must always keep in the forefront one question: What type of a caregiver, person or parent do I want to be? If you get stuck, ask for help, see a counselor, do what you have to do to live a brilliant life for you and your child.

Sometimes half the battle is knowing how you feel. Here is a coping tip I learned from a counselor who helped me through a particularly hard time. I wish I had known how to do it earlier. It is pretty simple.

First give the feelings that are causing the most pain a name, example if you feel anger call it anger. Then after your feeling has a name, ask yourself: "While feeling this "anger" can I have, do or be who I want to be?" Of course, the answer is no. This technique doesn't take the feeling away but it makes your feeling more manageable and the feeling doesn't have all the power to control you.

For you to be your child's #1 caregiver, your child's "Rock", you must learn how to take care of yourself first. If you are run down, not eating right or getting exercise, how can you effectively be there for those who need you the most?

I can't live in the "Oh My God my son is dying" space. It isn't my personality or mission in life. From that horrifying space I can't be the person I am or want to be. I can't be the mother, wife, care taker or citizen who lives in the troughs of constant negativity and debilitating grief. It would kill me and it would not set a good example to my children or others.

I look at my son's Duchenne as a "sacred journey" that we are taking together that hardly any other parent gets to take with their child. It is the highest honor that can be given to any parent. Many new age thinkers including myself believe our soul chooses our life path here on earth. I have also heard that the most sought after "earth lives" are special needs and challenged bodies so the soul can expand.

I surround myself daily with uplifting words like inspiration, hope, and miracle. On my desk is a card I framed in a gold frame that says "Cherish Today." On my living room wall I have two plaques. One reads "The Beauty of Life is to Live" and the other says "The Adventure of Life is to Learn." I try to live my life by these words. You will also find butterflies on almost every wall of my house. I have read about Holicost victims scratching thousands of butterflies into the walls of the gas chambers as butterflies are symbols of transformation and living on even after death. I hold onto this.

I also keep good company with like minded people so when the dark night of Duchenne is in my face and I can't breathe, they can be there to help give me strength to move into the pain knowing it is safe. How else are you supposed to feel about the assault of Duchenne on your child's body and your life?

While flipping through old journals and books I have read while preparing to write this book, I came across a letter my family support worker Gwen wrote me. Here is an excerpt I thought I'd share, smiley faces and all.

> *"Misty, you make me feel very competent as a*
> *parent and a family support worker. :) I'm very*
> *thankful for the day I first heard your name. Thank*
> *you for sharing your family with me. I am truly*
> *humbled when I see you playing with your*
> *children."*
> *Gwen :)*

People like Gwen help me pass through the eye of
the needle of pain. They help me see beauty to
reach beyond and expect more out of life.

Onward

Luke Delia Class of 2010

I am completely blessed to not only be Luke's mom but to be his friend. Over the years we have been put in circumstances where I had to be so much more than a "normal mom." I am his confidant, a person he can be who he is with, a person he has gone the distance with, and a person who has stood by his side during the horrors of Duchenne.

With each stage of this disease, there are lots of little deaths, each bringing new grief, new fears, new challenges and having to let go of once was. From walking to a wheelchair, from being able to dress yourself to someone else having to do it for you, from being able to bring the fork to your mouth to having to be fed. The simple things we take for granted disappear. It's often like taking one step forward and 3 steps back. The three steps back always taking you to the very same place. Duchenne Muscular Dystrophy is stealing your son's life. Somehow you have to go on with each downward progression to find the life balance that each of us desire without being swallowed whole from the shear and ever present, agonizing grief. I have often wondered when is it ever going to end just to realize if it did Luke wouldn't be here.

Yes, Duchenne sucks! So now what?

"Here I am Living For Today...But I'm Gonna Hope for Tomorrow" Expert From The Song Innocence by: Duchenne Music Project

Hope is what you have before dreams and miracles become reality. Now is the time to do, to take action, to push and live *ONWARD!*

At this very moment there are boys and young men dying of Duchenne. There are also boys and young men living and even improving the symptoms of Duchenne with treatments that for some reason are being hush hushed. I do understand we must make sure that treatments are safe and viable. It's hard to make rash decisions when our sons' lives are at stake, but isn't it high time to put the cure for Duchenne on the map?

With hesitant excitement Luke will be receiving his first STS treatment by Dr. Rhodes in June. Its a relatively new innovative treatment that works at the cellular level, with no harmful side effects. If I had it my way I would put Luke on the first plane out of Alaska. But Luke has decided to finish his senior year and graduate in May. He told me, "I need to put graduation behind me and the treatment will give me something to look forward too."

Does this scare me? Absolutely! But I force myself every day not to dwell on the negative. It is uncharted territory. Polio is a thing of the past and the cancer that President Carter declared war on is being cured everyday. What can't be done is always being done by someone, so why not a cure for Duchenne?

Below is an email I received from some dear friends of mine. I was expressing to them my fear of getting excited about this new treatment.

This email is their response:

Hi Misty,
Go ahead and get excited. You have committed your heart already (with some reservation, but you committed it when you decided to try this).
Faith and hope is the other part of the equation that makes any healing work. If it doesn't work, then that is what you have us for. You can rant and rave your frustrations and disappointments on us!
We pray that this new strategy will work, but why not expect miracles? I know that you have hoped against hope many times before, and have had some successes and some failures. In this world we do know miracles happen. They are rare, so we tend to think we are not worthy of them. That is correct logic, for none of us are worthy of them - even those who have had the miracles!
Miracles have happened to those without hope, without conscious belief, but that is even rarer. Go ahead and hope (with some reservation, but

recognize it is hope). Get excited (with some reservation, but get excited). The last verse in 1 Corinthians 13 says that "these three remain, faith, hope, and love, but the greatest of these is love." I know you already "love" so you already have the greatest ingredient for a miracle to happen.

The next is to simply believe the impossible. That is why we are all fools, but it is better to be a fool with hope, than a wise person in despair. Despair gets little done and is our biggest enemy...

We love you all and share in your hopes and your dreams.

We have some reservations, too, but we are excited!

Tim and Kelly Caraway

Will the treatment work? I must believe and "know" it will. High emotional stakes are at risk. For my husband who wants to fix this for Luke but can't. For Luke's siblings who cherish the ground he rolls his wheelchair on. For the family, for Luke's dad's family, for my daughter who had this to say about the treatment: "You mean that Luke could one day hug me back?"

And for me, although there is a certain amount of comfort and "normalness" in living this long with Duchenne I am thrilled to be in this spot, living and watching Luke live. But I have to admit it scares the absolute shit out of me to change the dance steps and head into the uncharted territory of Luke living a very long time. Have I done what is best for Luke? Have I taught him enough about self advocacy for him to be able to live an independent life?

Unequivocally YES! Why, because that is what mom's do.

In Your Face, Duchenne Muscular Dystrophy, All Pain...All GLORY!

Postscript, Meant To Be

I have been led if you will to the right people just when I need them. As if some magical force or being is guiding me, directing my destiny if there is such a thing. I get goose bumps and tears instantly spring to my eyes even now relating this to you my reader.

Synchronicity has manifested in my life from the start of meeting my husband Glen and finding out I was born in the farm driveway, my knowings of medical facts relating to Luke and Duchenne, the lovely birth of "my girl" Jenna and now the timing of events that lead to writings of "In Your Face." Which still are continually happening.

The minute I had the title, most of the words just "fell out of me." Every time I asked for internal guidance what I needed appeared. Like meeting Debra Miller at CureDuchenne, even finding the perfect editor was effortless. Not to say there weren't times I had to put my writing aside to step out the pain long enough to rejuvenate or deal with life and Luke's disability/medical issues or that I didn't go within and ask for guidance, because I did. Then came the perfect timing of the Internet marketing course Crowd Conversion on how to use Facebook for authors which gave me the fundamentals and the tools to proceed into a successful pre-launch.

The most current serendipitous event was I knew I needed help with my website and marketing "In Your Face" I asked to be shown the way. A few days later Kimberly Bohannon from Go For Your Dream contacted me to be apart of her wonderful 12 month case study to teach me how to polish my world wide web presence with a professional website and blog that gives justice to both the book and the Duchenne Movement. "Ask and believe and you shall receive", try it, it really works.

The entire roller coaster of everything that has ever happened to me was a stepping stone that has led to this very moment, including the double edge sword of Duchenne. What can I say "In Your Face" Was meant to be.

Endnotes

Chapter One

Alaska Parenting Magazine (no longer in publication) ei http:// Frontiersman.com

Chapter Three

"You Can Heal Your Life" by Louise Hay; (Hay House Inc. 1987)

Chapter Four

Muscular Dystrophy Association http// MDA.org

Parent Project Muscular Dystrophy http:// ParentProjectMd.org

Make-A-Wish http:// MakeAWish.com

Chapter Five

Run for our Sons http:// RunForOurSons.org

Partners in Policy Making, 2005 "changing the way people with disabilities are supported, viewed, taught, live and work since 1987" http"// PartnersInPolicyMaking.com

Chapter Eight

2007 Mastery of the Heart Phone Conference Program by Diana Vela Founder and Director of he Heart Inc. http:// ProgramsOfTheHeart.com

Dr. Oz May 21 2007 Oprah Show, Energy Medicine, "the new frontier of medicine"

Healing Codes http:// MistyVanderWeele.com

Onward

"Innocence" Duchenne Music Project http:// MySpace.com/ DuchenneMusicProject

Dr. Rhodes, STS Units, http:// PainDefeat.com

Join the Duchenne Movement, wear the T-Shirt

(Lime Green Duchenne Awareness Ribbon with Black writing, BACK)
Wording on back, "Stop the 20,000 being diagnosed every year"

(Lime green awareness Ribbon Logo on FRONT)

Order Yours Today!

http://www.MistyVanderWeele.com